D1635430

OFFICIAL TEXT

THIS IS HISTORY!

'King' Cromwell?

A KEY STAGE 3 DEPTH STUDY

ANDY
HARMSWORTH

IAN
DAWSON

The Schools History Project

The Project was set up in 1972, with the aim of improving the study of History for students aged 13–16. This involved a reconsideration of the ways in which History contributes to the educational needs of young people. The Project devised new objectives, new criteria for planning and developing courses, and the materials to support them. New examinations, requiring new methods of assessment, also had to be developed. These have continued to be popular. The advent of GCSE in 1987 led to the expansion of Project approaches into other syllabuses.

The Schools History Project has been based at Trinity and All Saints College, Leeds, since 1978, from where it supports teachers through a biennial Bulletin, regular INSET, an annual conference and a website (www.tasc.ac.uk/shp).

Since the National Curriculum was drawn up in 1991, the Project has continued to expand its publications, bringing its ideas to courses for Key Stage 3 as well as a range of GCSE and A level specifications.

Note: The wording and sentence structure of some written sources have been adapted and simplified to make them accessible to all pupils, while faithfully preserving the sense of the original.

Words printed in SMALL CAPITALS are defined in the Glossary on page 66.

© Andy Harmsworth and Ian Dawson 2002

First published in 2002
by John Murray (Publishers) Ltd, a member of the Hodder Headline Group
338 Euston Road
London NW1 3BH

Reprinted 2004

Layouts by Amanda Hawkes
Artwork by Art Construction, Neil Chapman, Jon Davis (Linden Artists), Richard Duszczak, Tony Randell, Edward Ripley (Linda Rogers Associates), Steve Smith
Typeset in Goudy, by Wearset Ltd, Boldon, Tyne and Wear
Printed and bound in Spain by Bookprint, S.L., Barcelona

A catalogue entry for this book is available from the British Library

Pupils' Book ISBN 0 7195 8559 7
Teachers' Resource Book ISBN 0 7195 8560 0

◆ Contents

MARCH 1657

HEAR, HEAR!

HEAR, HEAR!

Oliver Cromwell, we would like you to be our king.

Oliver Cromwell is a great man. He has led us through the Civil War, the most dangerous times in our history. Thanks to him, we defeated all our enemies. Now, after all the war and bloodshed, we have a chance for peace and prosperity under his wise leadership!

DISCUSS

1 Study the left-hand picture. Choose three words that sum up what people thought of Oliver Cromwell in 1657.
2 Now study the right-hand picture. Choose three different words that sum up what people thought of him in 1661.
3 Can you think of any reasons why people might have changed their minds about Oliver Cromwell?

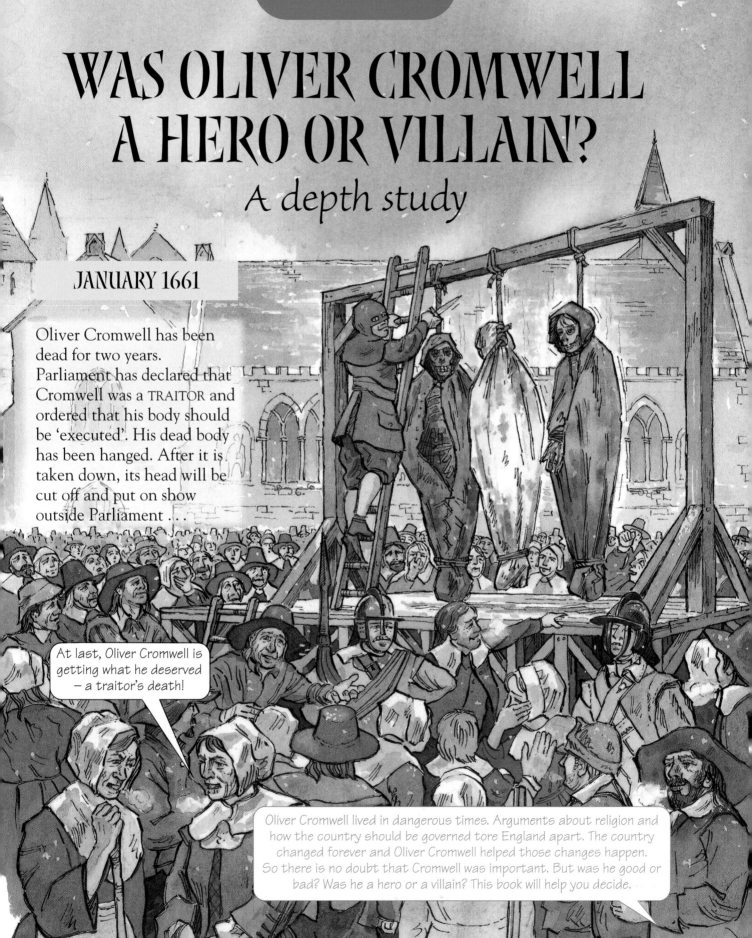

WAS OLIVER CROMWELL A HERO OR VILLAIN?

A depth study

JANUARY 1661

Oliver Cromwell has been dead for two years. Parliament has declared that Cromwell was a TRAITOR and ordered that his body should be 'executed'. His dead body has been hanged. After it is taken down, its head will be cut off and put on show outside Parliament . . .

At last, Oliver Cromwell is getting what he deserved – a traitor's death!

Oliver Cromwell lived in dangerous times. Arguments about religion and how the country should be governed tore England apart. The country changed forever and Oliver Cromwell helped those changes happen. So there is no doubt that Cromwell was important. But was he good or bad? Was he a hero or a villain? This book will help you decide.

◆ *The Cromwell quiz*

You may know lots about Oliver Cromwell already. You may know nothing. This quiz will test your knowledge *and* help you see why Cromwell is CONTROVERSIAL.

ᴀC T I V I T Y ᴀ

Work with a partner. Study each of Cromwell's decisions. Discuss the advantages and disadvantages of each option. Then decide which option you think Cromwell chose. This may just be a guess. It doesn't matter if you are wrong. Keep a note of your choices – you'll need them later.

DECISION 1
1642: Who to fight for?
Civil war broke out in England. Did Cromwell:
a) wait to see who was winning the Civil War, then join that side to further his own career
b) stay neutral because war would be a disaster for England
c) fight against the King to force him to share power with Parliament?

DECISION 2
1648: What to do with the King?
King Charles lost the Civil War. Did Cromwell:
a) murder King Charles himself and take over as king
b) put King Charles in prison for the rest of his life
c) put King Charles on trial for TREASON, then execute him when he was found guilty?

DECISION 3
1649: Mercy or slaughter?
Cromwell was sent to Drogheda in Ireland to stop a REBELLION. Did Cromwell:
a) order his soldiers to attack the town and kill everyone in it
b) go into Drogheda himself to persuade the people to surrender
c) order his soldiers to kill enemy soldiers but protect innocent civilians?

DECISION 4
1653: Abolish Christmas?
Some religious people abolished Christmas because it was not mentioned in the Bible. Did Cromwell:
a) support the ban
b) stay neutral because it was not really a very important issue
c) oppose the ban – because everyone has the right to have some fun at Christmas?

DECISION 5
1657: King Oliver?
Cromwell was the most powerful person in England. MPs asked him to become king. Did Cromwell:
a) accept their offer at once – it was what he'd always wanted
b) delay a decision while he prayed about it and consulted his supporters in the army
c) turn them down at once and tell them not to be so stupid – England had got rid of monarchy for good?

ACTIVITY B

This activity is one that you start now but you will come back to it several times later on. Look back to your answers to the quiz opposite.

◆ If you picked mostly **a** you think **Cromwell was a villain**.
◆ If you picked mostly **c** you think **Cromwell was a hero**.
◆ If you picked a mixture of **a**, **b** and **c** then you think that **Cromwell was sometimes a hero and sometimes a villain**.

This is your hypothesis. A hypothesis is an idea to be tested. As you work through pages 6–43 you will collect evidence to see if your hypothesis is right. You will find out what Cromwell actually did in these situations. Fill in the Hero or Villain scales after each unit, to record the evidence. At the end of the book you will have to weigh up the evidence and decide which hypothesis is right.

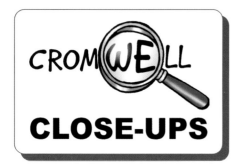

CLOSE-UPS

At the end of Section 1 you will write your own biography of Cromwell. A biography is a piece of writing about someone's life. Biographies are one of the most popular forms of history.

You will get lots of advice on writing your biography on pages 48–54. But there are two basic rules for writing a good biography:

Rule 1: Study the evidence

Like all good historians you need to study the evidence and base your conclusions on what you find.

Rule 2: Get to know your character

The more you know about the character, the easier it will be to write in an interesting way about him or her.

To help you get to know Cromwell, here are some 'Cromwell Close-ups'. There will be more of them later in the book.

1 This portrait of Cromwell was painted by Samuel Cooper around 1650 when Cromwell was the most powerful man in Britain. Cromwell told Cooper, 'Paint my picture exactly like me and do not flatter me at all. Show all these wrinkles, pimples, warts and everything else as you see me. Otherwise I will not pay a farthing for it.'

2 He enjoyed country activities, like horse-riding and hunting with hawks. He was a very good horseman.

3 He was emotional and moody, especially when he was a young man. He had a bad temper. He could get very angry with people who disagreed with him. He could be very rude to them and stamp his feet on the floor. Afterwards he would break down into floods of tears.

4 He liked honesty and plain-speaking. In 1654 he began an important speech to MPs by saying, 'I shall exercise plainness and freeness with you.'

5 Cromwell was a scruffy dresser. When he made a speech to Parliament in 1640, another MP said that he was wearing a cheap, ordinary suit, his shirt was not very clean and there were some specks of blood on his collar (from where he had cut himself shaving).

1590	1600	1610

1599 born

6 As a young man, Cromwell often lay awake at night thinking that he was dying. In 1628 he visited a famous London doctor, Theodore Mayerne. The doctor wrote that Cromwell was 'extremely melancholy'; a modern doctor would probably say that Cromwell was suffering from depression.

7 When he first went to Parliament, he made lots of gaffes (silly mistakes). Many MPs did not really trust him. He was impulsive, rushing in when a wiser person might have stopped to think first, and naïve. He could not understand why other people disagreed with him.

8 When Cromwell went to fight in the Civil War, he was 43 years old. He had never been a soldier before. But he enjoyed the danger and excitement of war. People said that he always had a beaming smile on his face when he charged into battle.

9 Sometimes Cromwell could not decide what to do. He agonised for weeks over some important decisions, even making himself ill. At other times, however, he seemed to know instantly what to do and exploded into action.

10 Cromwell made many enemies. They said that he was cruel, ruthless and totally selfish. Cromwell always denied this. He said that he always acted in the country's best interests and followed God's will.

ACTIVITY

These activities will help you to write your biography of Cromwell later on.

1 Your questions
Brainstorm some questions about Cromwell and write them down. Look out for answers to them as you work through Section 1.

2 Cromwell word bank
Build up a bank of words or phrases that bring Cromwell to life. They could be words people have used to describe him, or words that you think of yourself. You could put them in three lists according to their attitude towards Cromwell:

◆ positive words
◆ negative words
◆ neutral words.

You could do this as a class. Stick three large sheets of paper on the wall. Write your words on the sheets as you think of them.

To start you off, choose some good words to describe Cromwell from Close-ups 1–9. Add words to your word bank as you work through this book. Remember to cross out any words that you no longer agree with, as you find out more about Cromwell.

3 Your timeline
Build up your own timeline of Cromwell's life. This will be very useful when you write your biography. Here are some basic details to get you started. Add more details to your own copy as you work through Section 1.

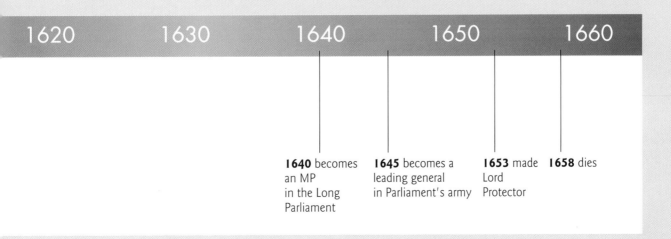

| 1620 | 1630 | 1640 | 1650 | 1660 |

1640 becomes an MP in the Long Parliament

1645 becomes a leading general in Parliament's army

1653 made Lord Protector

1658 dies

WHY DID CROMWELL GO TO WAR?
Get inside Cromwell's mind as he decides whether to fight against the King

Welcome to 1640. Parliament is meeting for the first time in eleven years. Some MPs are angry. I'm here to find out why. I have just met one of the new MPs, Oliver Cromwell. And here he is! I am going to ask him some questions . . .

ACTIVITY

The MP about to be interviewed is Oliver Cromwell. You have to write Cromwell's answers for him. Over the next eight pages you will find the information you need. The page references tell you where to look. You can then write out your answers or record your interview on tape.

1 What is your name and where do you come from? **(pages 6–7)**

2 Most MPs seem to be very worried about religion. How important is religion to you? **(page 8)**

3 Do you want the Church of England to be more Catholic or more Puritan? **(pages 8–10)**

4 Do you think Roman Catholics are a danger to England? **(page 11)**

5 Do you think the King was right to rule the country without Parliament? **(pages 12–13)**

6 Do you think that King Charles has made any mistakes in the past eleven years? **(pages 12–13)**

7 What do you most want King Charles to do now? **(page 13)**

◆ Young Cromwell

1599
Cromwell was born in Huntingdon in 1599. His father was a farmer. They were well off but not rich.

1612
Oliver was clever. His father sent him to the local grammar school. His teacher was Dr Beard. The pupils spent most of their time being taught about religion. Dr Beard told them that God was always watching them and sent signs to tell them what to do. He beat the pupils when he thought they were being lazy.

1617 Oliver went to Cambridge University to study law when he was seventeen. Soon afterwards his father died. Oliver had to give up his studies to look after his mother and six sisters.

1620 In 1620 Oliver married. He and his wife Elizabeth were very happy. When the rest of his life was hard, his home life always made him feel secure.

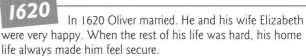

1631 Cromwell was short of money. He had to move his family to a smaller house. At about this time he fell ill and nearly died. Later he said that God had helped him through this terrible time. He believed God had made him a stronger person.

1636 In 1636 Oliver's rich uncle died and left him all his land. Oliver, Elizabeth and their six children moved to live in his large house in Ely. Oliver was now one of the richest men in his county. He believed God had rewarded him for his struggles.

1640 In 1640 Oliver was chosen to be the MP for Cambridge in the new Parliament. He was glad to do his duty. He was worried about the way King Charles had been making the churches more colourful and decorated.

ACTIVITY

This is a reminder of the activities that were introduced on pages 3 and 5. We won't keep reminding you later in the book.

1 Does this story strip give you any evidence to add to your Hero or Villain scales?
2 What words can you add to your word bank? Would any of these help you:
religious; hard-working; lazy; clever; ordinary; dutiful; selfish; fun-loving?
3 Add details to your timeline of Cromwell's life.
4 There is an anachronism on page 6. What is it?

◆ Why was religion so important to Oliver Cromwell?

To understand Cromwell you have to understand his religion. His religious beliefs were more important to him than anything else.

In the 1600s most people in Britain were very religious. Everyone was a Christian. They went to church every Sunday and at other important times of the year such as Easter. They believed that if they did the right things and worshipped God in the right way they would go to Heaven when they died. Therefore religion was important to everybody.

The trouble was that people disagreed about what kind of Church to have. In the Middle Ages, up until the early 1500s, everything had been simple. There was only one kind of Christianity – the Roman Catholic Church. But in 1534 Henry VIII broke away from the Roman Catholic Church and set up the Church of England. This became a Protestant church.

By the middle of the sixteenth century a tug-of-war had started between Catholics on one side and Puritans, who were extreme Protestants, on the other. Each wanted to pull the Church of England in its direction. These two pages show you what they were arguing about.

ROMAN CATHOLIC

I am a Roman Catholic. Mine is the true religion. I believe that:

- the Pope in Rome is the true head of the Church
- bishops help the Pope to control the Church
- the Bible and church services should be in Latin
- churches should be beautifully decorated with wall paintings, statues and stained-glass windows
- priests should wear richly decorated robes
- priests should not marry; they should devote their lives to God instead.

We celebrate the great Christian festivals such as Christmas and Easter.

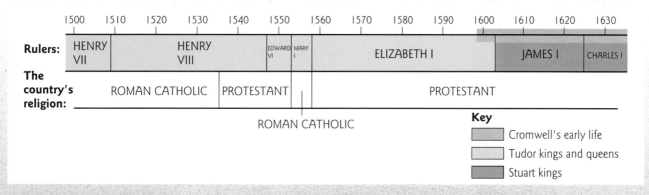

Rulers:	HENRY VII	HENRY VIII	EDWARD VI	MARY I	ELIZABETH I	JAMES I	CHARLES I

The country's religion:

ROMAN CATHOLIC   PROTESTANT   PROTESTANT

ROMAN CATHOLIC

Key
- Cromwell's early life
- Tudor kings and queens
- Stuart kings

DISCUSS

1 What do you think the Roman Catholics disliked about the Church of England?

2 What did Puritans dislike about the Church of England?

3 Do you think the Church of England sounds more Catholic or more Puritan?

4 Which group do you think Oliver Cromwell belonged to?
(Look back to page 7 if you need clues.)

MODERATE PROTESTANT

I am an ANGLICAN. I support the Church of England. In this country's church:

- the King or Queen is the Head of the Church
- bishops help the King or Queen control the Church
- the Bible is in English
- some ornaments and decoration are allowed
- priests must wear coloured robes
- priests are allowed to marry.

We also celebrate the great Christian festivals such as Christmas and Easter.

EXTREME PROTESTANT

I am a Puritan. I believe that:

- God is the true head of the Church, not the King with his bishops
- the Bible and church services should be in English
- churches should be completely plain
- priests should not wear colourful robes
- priests can marry

Festivals such as Christmas and Easter should be abolished because they are not mentioned in the Bible.

◆ Why did the Puritans distrust the Catholics?

Cromwell was a Puritan. At school he was taught by Dr Beard who was also a Puritan. These are some of the things that Dr Beard might have taught young Oliver when he was the same age as you.

> The Roman Catholic religion is the Church of the Devil. We must purify the Church in England to get rid of the Catholic ways. We want it to be like the simple Church of the Bible.

> We don't need priests or bishops in fancy, colourful robes. Our church leaders are just ordinary people who know the Bible. They can marry. They dress simply.

> Get rid of stained-glass windows and statues. People end up worshipping the decorations instead of worshipping God!

> Ban Catholic festivals like Christmas and Easter. They are not mentioned in the Bible!

> Make Sunday the Lord's day. Sundays are for thought and prayer – not for sports, games or going to the theatre!

> Help people live holier lives so they can get to Heaven. Stop drinking, swearing and gambling. That is the Devil's work!

> **1** What would happen if the King or Queen were Catholic? God help this country if that should ever happen! Learn these lessons from history, Oliver . . .

> **2** In 1553 Queen Mary tried to make England Catholic. She burned 300 Protestants at the stake. Only a few brave Protestants stayed true to our religion.

> **3** When Elizabeth was Queen, Catholics plotted to kill her. In 1588 King Philip of Spain sent his Armada to attack England and replace Elizabeth with a Catholic.

> **4** Then, Oliver, in 1605 – you might even be able to remember this from when you were a small boy – the Catholics tried to blow up Parliament and kill the King and all the Lords and MPs. They hated King James because he was a Protestant and wanted to replace him with a Catholic.

> **5** God gave us the victory each time but we must NEVER rest!

ACTIVITY

1 Match Sources 1–3 with each of Dr Beard's three warnings from history (see bubbles 2–4 on page 10).
2 Use pages 8–11 to write your answers to questions 2–4 on page 6.

SOURCE 1

SOURCE 2

SOURCE 3

◆ Why were MPs angry with the King?

ACTIVITY

You should have answered the reporter's first four questions on page 6 by now. The next three are about the King and Parliament.

1 To answer questions 5–7, you have to work out why MPs were angry with the King in 1640. Read pages 12–13 and fill in your copy of the table below. We've helped you with the first two topics by colour-coding them. For topics 3–5 you are on your own!
  ◆ The phrases in blue show you what Charles did.
  ◆ The phrases in green show you why Charles thought he was right.
  ◆ The phrases in red show you why MPs were angry.

Issues	What Charles did	Why Charles thought it was right	Why some MPs were angry about this
Parliament			
Taxes			
Religion			
Wentworth			
Scotland			

2 Use your completed table to help you write Cromwell's answers to questions 5–7 on page 6.
3 You could now transfer your whole interview on to video or audio tape.
4 If you had been an MP in 1640, what changes would you have wanted to the way Charles was ruling the country?

IMPORTANT – READ THIS FIRST!

How was England governed in the seventeenth century?

Kings and queens did not have to call Parliament. They used Parliament to approve taxes for war or make new laws. The monarch was far more important than Parliament.

Parliament had been growing more important since it helped Henry VIII to change the country's religion. MPs expected the king to listen to their advice but they knew that he would still make his own decisions.

Parliament

In 1625, King Charles asked Parliament to agree to raise taxes to pay for a war against Spain but MPs refused. They did not trust Charles. After many years of arguments, Charles sent the MPs home (closed Parliament) in 1629. MPs were angry because they thought the King should rule with the help of Parliament. Instead, he ruled without Parliament for eleven years. Later on, MPs called this time the Eleven Years' Tyranny. But Charles believed that God had chosen him to be king and so Parliament should do what the king said.

Taxes

Parliament would not raise money for Charles so he ordered all landowners to pay Ship Money. Ship Money paid for the navy. In the past, only people near the coast paid it. But Charles said that, as the navy protected everyone in England, everyone should pay it. Most people did pay but one landowner, John Hampden, refused. He said that Ship Money was against the law because Parliament had not agreed to the tax. The King's judges sent him to prison for disobeying the King.

Religion

Charles' French wife, Henrietta Maria, was a Roman Catholic. Some people believed that Charles and the Archbishop of Canterbury, William Laud, were Catholics too because they encouraged priests to wear colourful robes. They also increased the number of statues and stained-glass windows in churches. MPs were Protestants who hated Catholic ideas.

Puritans protested about the changes but Charles ordered that three Puritan leaders be whipped through the streets of London, have their ears cut off, be branded with a red-hot iron and imprisoned for life.

Wentworth and Ireland

Charles wanted to control Ireland because it could be a threat to England. In 1633 he sent Sir Thomas Wentworth to take control of Ireland. In 1640 Charles promoted Wentworth to be his chief adviser and made him Earl of Strafford. But MPs did not trust Wentworth. They thought he was too powerful. They feared he would use an Irish army to arrest the King's enemies and close Parliament.

Scotland

Scotland had a Puritan Church. Charles hated it. In 1637 he tried to make it more like his Church of England. When the Scots protested, Charles sent an army to attack them. It was easily defeated and the Scots insisted Charles should pay them for the cost of the war. He had to call Parliament in 1640 to get this money. He needed MPs to agree to taxes being collected. MPs refused to do so, unless Charles agreed to change how he had been ruling the country.

◆ 1640: Compromise

Cromwell was one of 500 MPs who travelled to Westminster in November 1640. He was not well known. He supported John Pym, Parliament's leader. Pym said that Parliament should not let the King have any money unless he agreed to the following demands:

JOHN PYM

PYM'S DEMANDS

Call a Parliament for advice at least every three years

Close Parliament only if MPs agree

Collect taxes only with Parliament's permission

Reverse all the Catholic changes in the Church

Get rid of his main advisers, Strafford and Archbishop Laud

This was very risky. Some MPs were worried that standing up to the King like this was treason. They might be arrested or executed. Or worse, God might punish them (they believed the King was chosen by God). However, nearly all the MPs supported Pym's demands. The risk paid off. Six months later Charles had agreed to:

KING CHARLES

CHARLES' CONCESSIONS

Call a Parliament every three years and not end it without MPs' agreement

Make Ship Money illegal

Stop Archbishop Laud's changes and put him in prison

Execute the Earl of Strafford after Parliament had found him guilty of treason

ACTIVITY A

Look at the thought bubbles below. Which do you think is most likely to have been what Cromwell thought about King Charles' changes? (Look back to Cromwell's religious ideas before you decide.)

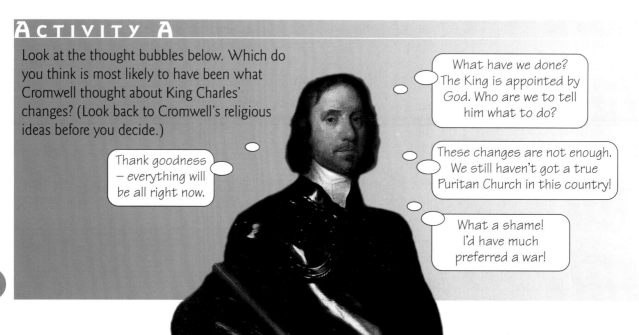

What have we done? The King is appointed by God. Who are we to tell him what to do?

Thank goodness – everything will be all right now.

These changes are not enough. We still haven't got a true Puritan Church in this country!

What a shame! I'd have much preferred a war!

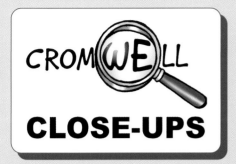

CLOSE-UPS

Cromwell in Parliament

We don't know much about Cromwell at this time. He was not an important MP in 1642 even though he became famous later, during the Civil War. But we do know about some of the speeches he made in Parliament. You can work out some things about him from these speeches.

Cromwell did not make speeches about the King's taxes or the way he ruled without Parliament.

His speeches were all about religion. He:

◆ protested about the punishment of Puritans
◆ wanted a new law to get rid of 'Catholic superstitions'
◆ wanted to abolish bishops.

Cromwell was still worried that the King wanted to force everyone to be a Catholic again, just like Mary Tudor had.

◆ *1642: War!*

By 1641 most MPs hoped that the country's problems were now over. It seemed that the King really wanted to work *with* Parliament, not against it. Yet one year later war had broken out between them. You are going to find out why...

ACTIVITY B

Your reporter is back again. Use the information on pages 16–17 to write Cromwell's answers to this new set of questions.

1 Did you think, in 1641, that the King would be able to work with Parliament?

2 What made you realise the problems were not over?

3 Why did Parliament decide to take control of the army?

4 Are you one of the most famous and important MPs?

1642

5 What were Parliament's final demands to the King?

6 Why were you worried about how the King's children were being brought up?

7 Why did some MPs fight for the King instead of for Parliament?

8 Why did you choose to fight against your King?

9 So – what are you going to do now?

ACTIVITY C

Remember to add details to your timeline and words to your word bank from pages 8–17.

◆ 1641–1642: Five steps to civil war!

1 November 1641

TERRIBLE NEWS FROM IRELAND!

A rebellion broke out in Ireland. Irish Catholics murdered thousands of Protestants. All the English MPs wanted to send an army to punish the Catholics but Parliament and the King could not agree about who should command it. Pym did not trust the King.

CHARLES

It is my right to command the army.

JOHN PYM

We can't allow the King to command the army. He might use it to close down Parliament. We must control the army!

2 January 1642

ARREST THOSE MEN!

The King took 400 soldiers to Parliament to arrest Pym and four other MPs. Charles burst into the House of Commons but the five MPs had escaped.

These men are traitors. They have been trying to destroy my powers. They must be punished.

I've been telling MPs for months that the King was trying to use soldiers to attack Parliament. That's why we must limit his power even more.

3 March 1642

PARLIAMENT TO TAKE OVER THE ARMY!

Pym and the other four MPs were treated like heroes in London. The King left the city and began gathering soldiers in the north of England.

Pym persuaded MPs to make a law giving Parliament control of the army. This was the first time in history that Parliament had ever made a law without the King's permission.

The King is preparing to attack Parliament. We must be able to defend ourselves!

Only kings can make laws and command the army. Pym must be stopped!

4 June 1642

PYM'S FINAL DEMANDS!

Pym sent Parliament's final demands to the King.

- The King's advisers must be approved by MPs.
- Parliament must control the army.
- Parliament should decide the future of the Church.
- Parliament should make sure the King's children are brought up as Protestants and decide how they are educated and who they marry.
- The King must get rid of his soldiers.

These are reasonable demands to protect Parliament and the Protestant religion. If the King accepts them, he can stop this war.

I can never accept these demands. They would destroy all the powers of the monarchy.

5 August 1642

IT'S WAR!

The King rejected Pym's demands and won the backing of 236 MPs. They thought that Pym had gone too far. They went north to join the King.

I order every county to provide soldiers to fight for me.

We order every county to raise soldiers to fight for Parliament.

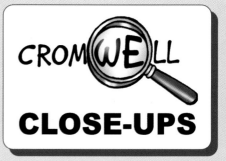

CROMWELL CLOSE-UPS

The start of the Civil War

In 1642 Cromwell was a middle-aged man who loved his family. He had never been a soldier. Although he disliked the way Charles had been ruling the country, he still thought the King was God's chosen ruler for England. So it's easy to think that Cromwell must have been in two minds about whether to fight against the King.

WRONG! Cromwell had no doubts at all. He left London for Cambridge in July to raise soldiers for Parliament. Cambridge University was sending money to help the King. Cromwell and his soldiers stopped them. This was a huge risk. Charles had not even declared war yet – as far as the King and his supporters were concerned, Cromwell was committing treason!

ACTIVITY

Remember to add evidence to your Hero or Villain scales from Unit 1.1.

Weigh up Cromwell's reputation as a brilliant army leader. Was he really that good?

ACTIVITY

Can you tell the story of the Civil War – and Cromwell's part in it? The drawings show you what happened – but we haven't written the story to go with the pictures. That's your job, using the information on pages 20–27 to help you!

Remember:

◆ It's up to you what you write – use the questions as a guide, don't just write a series of answers.
◆ You can write as much or as little as you like but make the story exciting!

1 1642

How did the war start? What was the King's aim?

2

Where was the first battle? What was the result?

3

Why did the ROYALISTS expect to win?

4

What advantages did Parliament have? Who was favourite to win the war?

5 1643

What kinds of men did Cromwell want in his army?

6

How did Cromwell treat his men? Did he turn them into good soldiers?

◆ *The two sides*

Charles declared war on Parliament at Nottingham on 22 August 1642. Then he marched south. His plan was to win the war with one knockout blow by capturing London. Parliament's main army blocked his path. The two armies met at the battle of Edgehill. The battle was a draw but 1500 men were killed.

This was a setback for King Charles. His advance on London was halted, but most people still thought that the King would win the war quickly. He set up his headquarters at Oxford, just 80 kilometres (50 miles) from London.

Key

- Areas controlled by Parliament in 1642
- Areas controlled by the King in 1642
- ▲ Parliamentary towns in 1642
- ■ Royalist towns in 1642
- ✕ Main battles

ROYALISTS
Nickname:
Cavaliers (cruel Spanish Catholic soldiers)

Commander:
King Charles I

Supporters:
Half the MPs, many landowners, many farm workers, Anglicans (supporters of the Church of England)

Parts of the country:
Northern England, the south-west and Wales. Many poor farming areas

Money:
Gifts of £2m from wealthy nobles

Armed forces:
About 25,000 soldiers. Good cavalry. Most soldiers were inexperienced and short of weapons and supplies

PARLIAMENT'S SUPPORTERS
Nickname:
Roundheads (short-haired London workers)

Commander:
The Earl of Essex

Supporters:
Half the MPs, many landowners, most merchants, shopkeepers and craftspeople, Puritans

Parts of the country:
South-eastern England, including London. Rich manufacturing and farming areas. Most of the ports

Money:
Short of money

Armed forces:
About 25,000 soldiers. Most of them were inexperienced and short of weapons and supplies

SCOTLAND

York
Marston ✕
Moor (1644) ■
Hull ▲

N

■ Chester

■ Nottingham

Shrewsbury ■

✕
Naseby (1645)

▲ Cambridge

✕ Edgehill (1642)

Gloucester ▲

Oxford

London ▲

Bristol ▲

Dover ▲

Portsmouth ▲

Exeter ■
Plymouth ▲

0 km   100 km

SOURCE 1 England during the Civil War.

ACTIVITY

1 Most people at the time thought that the Royalists were in a better position to win the war. Do you agree?

2 Complete frames 1–4 of your story strip.

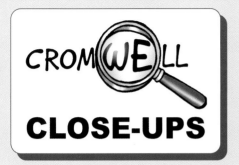

CROMWELL CLOSE-UPS

Did Cromwell become a good army commander?

After Edgehill Cromwell realised that Parliament needed more soldiers and they needed to be well equipped. He knew that cavalry were particularly important so he recruited his own army of over 1000 cavalrymen in East Anglia. Sources 2–6 tell you about Cromwell's skills as an army commander during the early stages of the war.

SOURCE 2 From a letter written by Cromwell in August 1643 to Parliament's officials in Suffolk. He is explaining the kind of officers he is looking for.

> I would rather have a plain-coated captain who knows what he is fighting for, and loves what he knows, than a rich gentleman who is nothing else.

SOURCE 3 From a letter Cromwell wrote to Oliver St John, a friend who also supported Parliament, in September 1643.

> I have a lovely company. They are honest Christians.

SOURCE 4 Richard Baxter, a Puritan churchman who supported Parliament, writing after the war.

> Cromwell had a special care to get religious men into his troop. This helped to avoid disorder, MUTINY and PLUNDER which soldiers are commonly guilty of.

SOURCE 5 From *Special Passages*, a newspaper published by Parliament, May 1643

> Cromwell has 2,000 brave and well disciplined men. If a man swears, he pays 12 pence [fine]. If anyone is drunk, he is set in the stocks or worse. If one calls the other 'Roundhead' he is thrown out. In the counties where they come, people jump for joy and join them. How happy it would be if all soldiers were so disciplined.

SOURCE 6 Barry Coward, a historian, wrote this in a biography of Cromwell in 1991.

> Cromwell fought several battles in 1643. He won them all. He controlled his men on and off the battlefield. He took them into battle in a close, tight formation. When they broke through the enemy's ranks, he did not allow his men to chase after them for plunder. Unlike other cavalry commanders, he regrouped his men and attacked the enemy from behind. These tactics proved devastatingly effective.

ACTIVITY

1 Read Sources 2–5. List all of the qualities that Cromwell was looking for in his soldiers.
2 Which do you think Cromwell would say was **the most important** quality?
3 a) How did Cromwell treat his men?
   b) Why did he treat his men this way?
   c) Was the way he treated his men successful?
4 Use these sources to help you write frames 5 and 6 of your story strip.

◆ *What was the fighting like?*

SOURCE 7 This is what battles were like in the seventeenth century.

Foot soldiers

Pikemen stood close together in battle. They pointed their pikes towards the enemy. This helped to protect their army against cavalry charges. About one-third of an army's foot soldiers were pikemen.

Musketeers usually fought in blocks, six rows deep. Three rows would fire their MUSKETS at the enemy while the others were reloading. Sometimes musketeers used a musket rest to support the musket when firing. This helped to improve the aim. Musketeers made up about two-thirds of an army's foot soldiers.

Pike – a wooden staff about 5 m long, with an iron point at the end. It was used against enemy cavalry.

Iron 'pot' helmet

Musket – it was only accurate over about 50 metres.

Round bag containing lead bullets

Woollen knee breeches

Artillery

In the seventeenth century, armies usually had between 10 and 20 heavy guns. They were expensive, heavy and difficult to transport, but could cause a lot of damage to the enemy. To fire them the gunner would pack the barrel with gunpowder and a cannonball, aim the cannon and then light the fuse. This took about 3 minutes.

ACTIVITY A

What can you learn from all the pictures about changes and continuities in warfare since the Middle Ages? Think back to your work on the battles of Hastings and Agincourt.

Cavalrymen

These charged in close formation into the enemy. They tried to chase the enemy cavalry from the battlefield. If the charge was successful, they would attack enemy foot soldiers from behind, surrounding them and then forcing them to surrender. But cavalrymen were difficult to reorganise after a charge.

Helmet with plates to protect the ears and neck

Leather gauntlets

Iron back and breast plates

Leather riding boots

Royalist forces charge the Parliamentarians during a re-enactment of the 'Battle of Powick', as part of the 350th anniversary celebrations of the First Civil War clashes in Worcester.

Reconstruction societies re-enact Civil War battles. Re-enactments like these are very popular today. The 'soldiers' use seventeenth-century battle tactics and copies of real Civil War weapons, uniforms and equipment. They study seventeenth-century sources to make sure that their re-enactments are as accurate as possible.

ACTIVITY B

It is August 1642. The war has just broken out. You are either King Charles or John Pym.

1 Make a list of what you will need to win the war, using these headings:

◆ types of soldiers
◆ weapons
◆ equipment
◆ supplies (think about what else your soldiers will need).

2 Why will you need money?
3 How are you going to get it?

23

◆ *Cromwell in action: The battle of Marston Moor*

Battle followed battle. Neither side was strong enough to win the war. Then came the biggest battle yet – the battle of Marston Moor – on 2 July 1644.

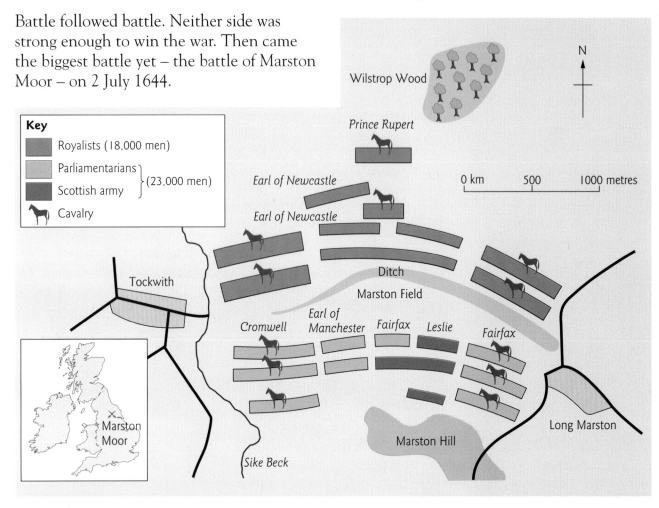

Key

	Royalists (18,000 men)
	Parliamentarians ⎫
	Scottish army ⎬ (23,000 men)
	Cavalry

Wilstrop Wood

Prince Rupert

Earl of Newcastle

Earl of Newcastle

N

0 km   500   1000 metres

Ditch

Marston Field

Tockwith

Earl of
Manchester

Cromwell

Fairfax   Leslie   Fairfax

Marston
Moor

Long Marston

Marston Hill

Sike Beck

SOURCE 8   The positions of the two armies when the battle started 6 km west of York. (An army of Scots had joined the war on Parliament's side in January 1644.)

The Earl of Newcastle's Royalist soldiers reached Marston Moor late in the afternoon. They were tired and hungry. They had been trapped in York by Parliament's forces since April. Prince Rupert, the Royalist commander, had fresh troops but he thought it was too late in the afternoon to fight.

Parliament's forces attacked at 7 o'clock that evening. Cromwell commanded 2500 cavalry from East Anglia. His men charged the Royalist cavalry in front of them. But Prince Rupert's cavalry attacked Cromwell's men. Cromwell was wounded in the neck, but regrouped his men, charged into Rupert's cavalry and scattered them.

On the other side of the battlefield, Parliament's cavalry were being beaten but Cromwell regrouped his men yet again and rode to help them. The Royalists fled from Cromwell's charge.

The foot soldiers were fighting fiercely in the centre. Then Cromwell's cavalry charged the Royalist foot soldiers. The King's men fought until they died, refusing to surrender. After two hours of fighting, Parliament had won an overwhelming victory. More than 4000 Royalist soldiers were killed and 1500 were taken prisoner. Only 300 of Parliament's soldiers were killed.

SOURCE 9 Two extracts from *The Rider of the White Horse* by Rosemary Sutcliff, 1959. One of Parliament's generals has ridden across the battlefield to find Cromwell and give him the bad news.

'The Right Wing's broken. There isn't a Right Wing any more and the Centre's going. B-Buccleuch and Loudon are broken. Maitland's lot are standing like heroes, and so are Lindsay's, but they can't last.'

Cromwell listened to him, his eyes blazing alive with a furious confidence in a face turned to grey iron. 'By God's help we are not yet beaten!' he said and wheeled his horse to gain the advantage of higher ground for a viewpoint.

It was for Cromwell to take the whole command, and Cromwell took it. Within half an hour the fortunes of the war had been turned completely inside out as the pattern of Marston Moor had been. For the army as a whole, he had ordered a wheel in line eastward across the moor. For himself, with a troop of sixty IRONSIDES [Parliamentary cavalry], followed by David Leslie and his Scots on their shaggy ponies, he had flung himself upon Goring's Horse [Royalist cavalry] and driven them from the field; then with Manchester's Infantry and Baillie's grim Scots, he turned on the last of Newcastle's Lambs [Royalist footsoldiers]. It was past dusk by now, but the moon was up in a clearing sky, watering the darkness with a wash of silver light; and the battle, for all its uproar, for all the yellow flame-flare of musketry, had become a struggling of shadows under the moon. Newcastle's Whitecoats retreated step by step to the old cattle enclosure on the moor behind them, as good a place as any other for a last stand. And there, an hour after, the Cause was lost; asking no quarter [refusing to surrender], the last stubborn pikeman went down fighting.

SOURCE 10 From a modern biography of Cromwell – *Cromwell, Our Chief of Men* by Antonia Fraser, 1973

The sky was already turning dark with an [approaching] storm, and soon after seven o'clock ominous claps of thunder were heard. Drenching rain now began to hail down on the heads of both armies. It was at this moment that on the Parliamentary left wing, Cromwell's well-tried men . . . began one of their new types of charges, rapid, controlled, riding short-reined and short-stirruped, close in together, probably at something like a fast trot rather than the modern gallop . . .

SOURCE 11 An extract from a letter Cromwell wrote to his brother-in-law two days after the battle.

Truly England and the Church of God had a great favour from the Lord in this great victory. God made them as stubble [stalks of corn] to our swords.

ACTIVITY

1 Complete this table.
2 Which sources are most useful for understanding
   a) what happened during the battle
   b) why Parliament won
   c) what battles were like to fight in?
3 Use these two pages to help you write frames 7–9 of your story strip.

Source	Type	What can I learn about the battle?
Main text	Our description	
Source 7 (pages 22–23)	Battle re-enactments	
Source 8	Plan of the battle	
Source 9	Novel	
Source 10	Biography	
Source 11	Cromwell's letter	

◆ *The New Model Army*

After the battle of Marston Moor, Parliament controlled the north of England. However, they could not beat the Royalists in the rest of the country. The trouble was that Parliament had many local armies instead of one national army. The local commanders could not agree about how to fight the war. Their men did not want to fight too far away from home.

Cromwell said that Parliament needed a new 'national' army and better generals. In 1645, MPs decided that Cromwell was right. They created the New Model Army – a national army of 22,000 men. MPs could order it to fight anywhere in the country. All its soldiers wore the same red uniform and were paid regularly. Its commander was Sir Thomas Fairfax, a Yorkshire landowner who was an excellent general. Cromwell was his deputy and commander of the cavalry.

On 14 June 1645 the New Model Army fought the Royalists at Naseby, near Northampton. Cromwell's brave cavalry charges helped Parliament to win a crushing victory. Five thousand Royalist soldiers were killed or captured. Afterwards, Cromwell told Parliament, 'This is the hand of God, and to Him alone belongs the glory.'

After Naseby it was clear to everyone that the King had lost the war. Charles finally surrendered in May 1646.

However, not everything had gone well for Cromwell. His eldest son, also called Oliver, had died in 1644 while fighting for Parliament.

ACTIVITY B

The New Model Army was one reason why Parliament won the war but it was not the only one. On the page opposite there is a summary of the different reasons.

Work in groups.

1 Make six cards, each one with a word or phrase to sum up the reasons on page 27 opposite.
2 Discuss why each reason helped Parliament to win.
3 Group the cards under the following headings: Resources, Money, Leadership, Soldiers, Religion. Colour each card, using a different colour for each group.
4 Take a piece of A3 paper and write 'Victory for Parliament' in one corner.
5 Now place the reasons on the A3 sheet. Put a reason close to the 'Victory' corner if **you** think it was very important in Parliament's victory. Put it further away if you think it was not important.
6 If you think any of the reasons are linked together, put them close together or overlapping.
7 Look at the pattern of the reasons. Where are the two Cromwell ones? The closer they are to the 'Victory' corner, the more important you think Cromwell was in giving Parliament victory.

Give Cromwell a mark out of ten for his importance. Giving him zero would mean he had nothing to do with it, while ten would mean he won the war single-handedly.

Now write a paragraph to explain your score.

ACTIVITY A

Use pages 26–27 to help you write frames 10–16 of your story strip.

◆ So why did Parliament win?

1 Parliament had better resources.

The King's strongholds were northern England, the south-west and Wales. These were mainly poorer farming areas. Parliament controlled the richer south-east of England, including London and the ports. And in 1644 a Scottish army came to fight for Parliament.

2 Parliament was better at collecting taxes to pay for its armies.

At the start of the war the King was given lots of money by his rich supporters but Parliament had no money of its own. By 1644 Parliament was collecting £1m a year to pay for its armies. The King was running out of money.

3 Cromwell was a brilliant cavalry commander.

In many battles – particularly the decisive ones at Marston Moor and Naseby – it was Cromwell's brave and well-organised cavalry charges that won the day. The *Perfect Diurnal*, a newspaper published by Parliament in 1645, said: 'God has miraculously chosen Cromwell as one of our saviours.'

4 Parliament had more soldiers than the Royalists at the most important battles.

At Naseby, Parliament had 14,000 soldiers against the King's 7500.

5 Cromwell and Fairfax created the New Model Army.

This was a national army. It was well led by Fairfax and Cromwell and was well trained and disciplined. It won the important battles at the end of the war.

6 God was on Parliament's side

Most of Parliament's soldiers were strong Puritans who believed God was on their side. This gave them a strong motivation to fight.

ACTIVITY C

Remember to add evidence from Unit 1.2 to your Hero or Villain scales.

A BLOODY MURDERER?

Write some conflicting interpretations of Cromwell's big decisions of 1649

The Civil War turned Cromwell into a famous and important man. Afterwards he became even more important. He was involved in every crisis and had to make hard decisions about England's future.

You can now investigate three of those decisions. Did Cromwell use his power to make the country a better place? Or was he a cruel and selfish DICTATOR using power for his own good?

ACTIVITY

1 Study at least two of the three investigations in Unit 1.3, working in pairs. You are going to write conflicting interpretations of Cromwell. One of you should write to show that Cromwell was a villain, the other to show that he was a hero.
2 Change roles for your second investigation.
3 Swap your work with another pair to see how good you are at spotting biased writing.

INVESTIGATION 1 Why did Cromwell execute King Charles?

One in ten men in England was killed during the Civil War. Thousands were wounded. Towns were looted, houses burned. By 1646, everyone wanted peace. MPs expected that the defeated king would agree to work with Parliament. Charles held talks with Parliament but he was really planning another war. In secret he made an agreement with certain Scottish supporters and in 1648 they invaded England to help Charles. This started the Second Civil War. MPs were furious. Cromwell led Parliament's army north to fight the Scottish force.

SOURCE 1 Cromwell speaking to army leaders about Parliament's talks with the King in July 1647.

> Whatever is achieved by such a treaty will be firm and lasting. Whatsoever is achieved by force will be weak.

SOURCE 2 Cromwell speaking to army leaders in April 1648, before fighting Charles' supporters.

> It is our duty, if ever the Lord brings us back in peace, to call Charles Stuart, that man of blood, to account for the blood he has shed.

DISCUSS

1 Did Cromwell want an agreement with the King in July 1647?
2 Did he still want an agreement in April 1648?
3 Did Cromwell's attitude towards the King change or stay the same?
4 Explain the likely reasons why.

Should the King be put on trial?

Cromwell's army faced the Scots at Preston in Lancashire, in August 1648. Cromwell won. The other army generals wanted Parliament to put the King on trial for treason and to execute him. Would Cromwell agree to this?

SOURCE 3 Cromwell's thoughts about the demands for King Charles to be put on trial and executed.

Royalists will be furious if the King is executed. Rebellions may break out all over the country. There will be even more bloodshed.

We could keep the King in prison. But there will be plots and rebellions to free him. Will this country ever be peaceful as long as he is alive?

The King is still popular with most of the people. They want the King and Parliament to work together. Is this the best way forward for England?

Can Charles be trusted? He talked peace before but then he deceived us and started another war. He might do that again.

Most MPs do not want to put the King on trial. They still want to reach an agreement with him.

Can I go against everything I have ever believed in? All my life I have believed that kings are appointed by God to rule this country.

The King has lost two wars. It must have been God's will for us to win and Charles to lose. So God has shown He is angry with Charles. God's will is clear. No one can deny God's will!

Can a king be put on trial? No one has ever done such a thing before. If I agree, Royalists will say I am a traitor.

DECISION TIME: DECEMBER 1648

Cromwell had two choices. He could:
  a) agree to put the King on trial and execute him, **or**
  b) support MPs' demands to carry on negotiating with the King.

1 Look at Cromwell's thoughts in Source 3. Which thoughts would lead him to option **a**? Which would lead him to option **b**?
2 From what you know already, which option do you think Cromwell chose – and why?
3 Read the next page.
   a) Which option did Cromwell actually choose?
   b) How certain was he about his decision?

The King's trial

The army leaders decided to put King Charles on trial but they knew many MPs were opposed to this. So they sent Colonel Pride to 'purge' Parliament by forcing all the MPs who were against the trial to leave Parliament. Out of 500 MPs only 154 were left. Cromwell was undecided until Christmas Day, when Charles rejected the army's last peace proposals.

SOURCE 4 Cromwell speaking in Parliament, late December 1648.

When it was first suggested that the King should be put on trial for treason, I thought that anyone who agreed was the greatest traitor in the world, but since God's will and necessity said it was right, I will pray for God to help them. We will cut off his head with the crown upon it.

The trial began on 20 January, but of the 135 men who had been chosen as judges only 68 turned up. Even Fairfax, the leader of the New Model Army, refused to take part. The chief judge, John Bradshaw, wore an iron hat for fear of being shot by a Royalist. Cromwell was one of the judges.

First the charge was read out:
'Charles Stuart was trusted to govern according to the laws and the good of the people. He is the author of the cruel and bloody wars; and guilty of all the treasons, murders and damage to this nation. He is therefore a tyrant, traitor and murderer, an enemy of the people of England.'

Charles refused to answer the charge. He said: 'I am your King. A king cannot be tried by any superior authority on Earth.'

He was taken away and tried in his absence. A week later he was found guilty and sentenced to death. Only 59 of the judges dared to sign the death warrant. Cromwell was the third to sign.

DISCUSS

1 Study Source 5. Can you find:
   a) the King handing his coat to his doctor
   b) the executioner showing the King's head to the crowd
   c) soldiers guarding the platform
   d) a woman fainting **e)** an old man crying
   f) the King's soul rising to heaven?
2 Do you think the artist was for or against the execution? What clues in the picture support your answer?
3 Why do you think Cromwell agreed to the trial and execution of the King – to get power for himself or for the good of the country?

The execution: Tuesday 30 January 1649

A special platform was built outside the King's palace in Whitehall. Huge crowds gathered around. They knew this was an important day. No one had executed a king before!

SOURCE 5 The King's execution, drawn soon afterwards by a Dutch artist. This is probably a reliable picture of where the scaffold was and what happened but it shows different things happening at the same time.

The weather was bitterly cold so Charles put on two shirts. He did not want to shiver as he went outside and have people say he was trembling with fear.

From the scaffold he made a speech. 'I did not begin a war with Parliament. They began these unhappy troubles. To the people I say, your freedom depends on having a government, not sharing in government. Remember.'

He placed his head on the block and the axe fell. One observer said, 'There was such a groan by the thousands present, as I never heard before and desire I may never hear again.'

Cromwell himself was not there. There are different accounts of where he was. One historian, Antonia Fraser, thinks the most likely explanation is that he was at a prayer meeting with his generals.

The King's body was put in an open coffin in a room in Whitehall Palace. Many people went to see it. According to a story first published 100 years later, one visitor muttered 'Cruel necessity' as he looked at the King's body. Some people think that the visitor was Oliver Cromwell, but no one knows for sure.

ACTIVITY

Now try the Activity introduced on page 28. Work in pairs.

a) **One of you** tell the story behind Source 5 to show that Cromwell was a bloodthirsty tyrant who wanted to get rid of the King.

b) **The other** tell it to show that Cromwell was a heroic leader who agreed to this extreme and horrible act only because he wanted to bring peace to England.

It doesn't matter which you believe yourself. It is sometimes quite a useful skill to be able to argue someone else's point of view.

Warning! There is one rule. Don't use the words 'hero' or 'villain' in your writing. You must find other words to express your viewpoint.

INVESTIGATION 2 Why did Cromwell shoot the Levellers?

After Charles was executed, England became a REPUBLIC. Parliament abolished the monarchy and the House of Lords. But the Levellers, led by John Lilburne, wanted even bigger changes. They wanted all men to vote in elections for Parliament.

Cromwell had already met the Levellers in 1647 to discuss their ideas. This discussion was called the Putney Debates.

SOURCE 6 Extracts from the Putney Debates, 1647.

1 The poorest person has a life to live, just like the richest. Any man who is born in England should have a vote in elections. He is not bound to obey a government if he has not had a voice to choose it.

Thomas Rainborough, a soldier

2 I do not think that just by being born here means a man should choose those who make the laws. No person hath such a right unless he owns land or a business.

Henry Ireton, an army general

3 Servants will try to destroy their masters if they are equal voters.

Colonel Rich, an army officer

4 We have been slaves. Now we want our freedom. Every person in England has a right to elect his representatives.

John Wildman, a civilian

5 We risked our lives to recover our rights, but we were deceived. The poor have preserved this kingdom. We will not lose that which we fought for!

Edward Sexby, a soldier

6 I was most dissatisfied with what I heard Mr Sexby speak.

Oliver Cromwell

ACTIVITY

Study the extracts from the Putney Debates in Source 6 on page 32 opposite.

1 Which speakers supported the Levellers?
2 Which speakers opposed them?
3 Who did Cromwell agree with?
4 What reasons did the Levellers give for 'one man, one vote'?
5 What reasons did their opponents give against it?

The Levellers did not get what they wanted in 1647. Two years later, after Charles' execution, they hoped that Parliament would accept their demands. But MPs rejected their ideas again. They thought the Levellers were a serious threat to their power.

The Levellers were angry. There were rumours that they were planning to seize power.

What should Cromwell do now? This was his dilemma:

1 Some of the Levellers' ideas are dangerous. Ordinary people should not be involved in politics. But some of their ideas are good. Like me, they want all good Protestants to be free to worship God as they please.

2 Our new republic is not yet safe. The dead king's son has proclaimed himself King Charles II. He is planning to gather support in Ireland to help him invade England. Many Royalists support him. If there is another war, I must have a strong and loyal army.

3 Many soldiers support the Levellers. They are very angry. Some people say that they are planning a rebellion.

4 Our new republic will not survive without the support of landowners. They hate the Levellers. They want me to destroy them.

5 We held talks with the Levellers two years ago. They failed. The situation is even more dangerous now.

SOURCE 7 Oliver Cromwell's thoughts about the Levellers in 1649.

DECISION TIME: MARCH 1649

Cromwell had two choices. He could:
a) crush the Levellers once and for all, **or**
b) hold some more talks with them.

1 Look at Cromwell's thoughts in Source 7. Which thoughts would lead him to option **a**? Which would lead him to option **b**?
2 What do you think Cromwell decided to do? Now read page 34 to see if you were right.

What did Cromwell do?

In March 1649, Cromwell and MPs decided to arrest the Leveller leaders for treason. They were imprisoned in the Tower of London. Two months later, 1000 soldiers, who supported the Levellers, rebelled. Cromwell did not hesitate. He and Fairfax gathered loyal troops and caught up with the rebels at Burford in Oxfordshire. They captured 400 rebel soldiers and shot three of their leaders.

Cromwell's quick and decisive action worked. There was no more trouble. The Leveller movement collapsed. Their idea of 'one man, one vote' was not heard again for nearly 200 years.

ACTIVITY

Now try the Activity introduced on page 28. Work in pairs. This picture shows the execution of the three Leveller rebels.

a) **One of you** tell the story in the picture to show that Cromwell was a bloodthirsty tyrant who did not want to share power with anyone.

b) **The other** tell it to show that Cromwell was a heroic leader trying to bring peace to England.

But **remember** – you can't use the words 'hero' or 'villain' in your writing.

INVESTIGATION 3 Why did Cromwell massacre the Irish?

Soon after he crushed the Levellers, Cromwell went to Ireland. What happened there is probably the most controversial part of Cromwell's story.

Why did Cromwell go to Ireland?

England had become Protestant in the 1530s. Ireland had stayed Catholic but English monarchs gave Irish land to Protestant settlers. Irish Catholics were furious. In 1641 they rebelled and killed thousands of Protestants (see page 16).

After Charles' execution, most Irish Catholics supported his son, Charles. They thought that he would protect their religion. Fearing trouble, Parliament sent an army under Cromwell's command to invade Ireland. From what you know about Ireland and about Cromwell, do you think he was likely to treat Irish Catholics fairly?

SOURCE 8 From a song, written 350 years later, by Irish group the Pogues.

A curse upon you, Oliver Cromwell,
You who raped our Motherland,
I hope you're rotting down in hell,
For the horrors that you sent,
To our misfortunate forefathers.

Cromwell landed with his army in August 1649. He needed to capture the enemy's nearest stronghold, Drogheda, quickly, or his expedition would fail. He had 12,000 soldiers. The town was strongly defended by 2500 of the enemy's best soldiers and 4000 civilians lived there too.

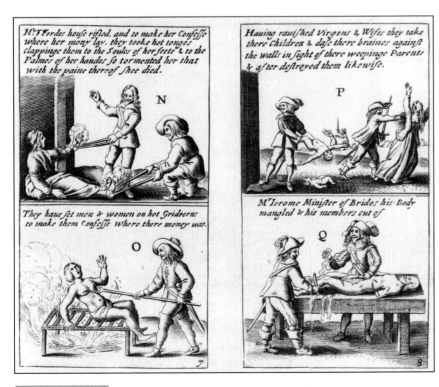

SOURCE 9 Incidents during the Irish Rebellion in 1641, drawn by a Protestant artist and printed in England.

DECISION TIME: 1649

Once his soldiers attacked Drogheda, Cromwell had five choices. He could:
a) give each defender one last chance to surrender
b) avoid bloodshed at all costs and take the defenders prisoner
c) kill everyone there (including women and children)
d) kill anyone carrying a weapon
e) kill only the Catholic priests.

1 Study Cromwell's choices. Think about the advantages and disadvantages of each option.
2 What would you advise Cromwell to do and why?

Dublin, 17th September 1649

Sir,

Your army came before the town of Drogheda on 3rd September. On Monday 9th the <u>battering guns</u> began to <u>play</u>. I sent Sir Arthur Aston, the Governor, a <u>summons</u> to <u>deliver</u> the town.

cannon — fire at the town

order — surrender

Receiving no satisfactory answer, the guns fired two or three hundred shot, beat down the corner tower, and opened up two reasonable <u>breaches</u> in the east and south walls.

big holes

Upon Tuesday the 10th, about five o'clock in the evening, we <u>began the storm</u> and after some hot fighting we entered, about seven or eight hundred men, the enemy disputing it very stiffly with us. Several of the enemy retreated to the Mill Mount [see Source 11], a place very strong and difficult to attack. The Governor, Sir Arthur Aston, being there, our men getting up to them were ordered by me to <u>put all to the sword</u>. And indeed, being in the heat of the action, I forbade them to spare any people who carried weapons in the town and I think that night they put to the sword 2,000 men.

attacked the town

kill all of them

Many of their officers and soldiers fled over the bridge into the other part of the town, where about 100 of them <u>possessed</u> St Peter's church steeple. These being <u>summoned to yield to mercy</u>, refused, whereupon I ordered the steeple of St Peter's Church to be <u>fired</u>. One of them was heard to say in the flames, 'God damn me, God confound me. I burn, I burn.'

told they would be treated well if they surrendered

went into

set on fire

The next day the other two towers were <u>summoned</u>, in one of which was about <u>six or seven score</u>. But they refused to <u>yield</u>. We knew that hunger must force them and set good guards to stop them running away. When they <u>submitted</u>, their officers were <u>knocked on the head</u> and every tenth man of the soldiers killed. The rest were captured.

120–140 soldiers

surrendered

asked to surrender

surrender

killed

The last <u>Lord's Day</u> before the storm, they had a <u>Mass</u> in St Peter's Church. About one thousand Catholics were put to the sword, fleeing there for safety. I believe all the <u>friars</u> were knocked on the head except two. One the soldiers <u>took</u> and <u>made an end of</u>. The other was captured in the round tower. He confessed he was a friar, but that did not save him.

Sunday

Catholic preachers captured

Catholic church service

killed

I believe that this is a <u>righteous</u> judgement of God upon these barbarous wretches, who have <u>dipped their hands in so much innocent blood</u>. And it will help to prevent more bloodshed in the future. It was God who gave your men courage. It is good that God has all the glory.

good

murdered many innocent people

I do not think we lost 100 men, though many be wounded.

Your most obedient servant,

Oliver Cromwell

SOURCE 10 Oliver Cromwell's report to Parliament about what happened in Drogheda.

SOURCE 11 A map of Drogheda in 1649.

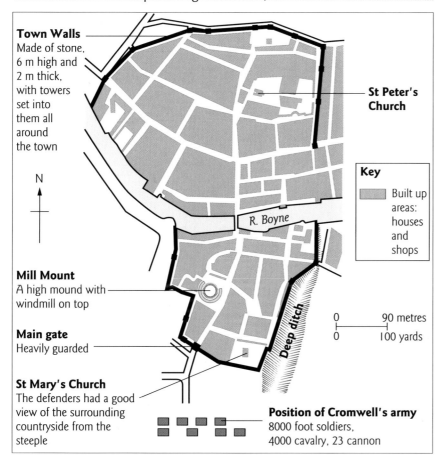

Town Walls
Made of stone, 6 m high and 2 m thick, with towers set into them all around the town

N

St Peter's Church

Key

Built up areas: houses and shops

R. Boyne

Mill Mount
A high mound with windmill on top

Deep ditch

0 ——— 90 metres
0 ——— 100 yards

Main gate
Heavily guarded

St Mary's Church
The defenders had a good view of the surrounding countryside from the steeple

Position of Cromwell's army
8000 foot soldiers, 4000 cavalry, 23 cannon

What happened afterwards?

After the attack on Drogheda, most other Irish towns surrendered without a fight. By the spring of 1650 Cromwell had conquered most of Ireland. When he returned to England, he was greeted as a hero.

ACTIVITY A

Now try the Activity introduced on page 28. Work in pairs.

a) One of you tell the story of Cromwell's attack on Drogheda to show that Cromwell was a bloodthirsty villain who murdered anyone who got in his way.

b) The other tell it to show that Cromwell was a heroic leader trying to make sure that England was safe from attack.

Remember: don't use the words 'hero' or 'villain' in your writing.

ACTIVITY B

1 Add evidence from this unit to your Hero or Villain scales.
2 Look at the interpretations your partner produced for Activity A.

   a) Pick out the words or phrases that show bias in his or her interpretation.
   b) Choose one example of bias that was easy to spot and one that was difficult.
   c) Why are some biased interpretations easier to spot than others?

Why did Cromwell turn down the chance to be king?

Parliament ruled the country for three years. But in 1653 the army generals asked Cromwell to take over. He became Lord Protector. In many ways he was a successful ruler. England became peaceful again. He took control of Ireland and Scotland. He made Britain stronger abroad. The navy defeated the Spanish and captured Jamaica in the West Indies.

In 1656, a new Parliament met. In 1657, MPs surprised Cromwell – they asked him to become King (see page iv)!

ACTIVITY

1 Cromwell did not keep a diary. This is a great pity. If he had, then we would understand a lot more about him and his decisions. So what you can see on these two pages is a recreated diary, based on other sources and events. Your task is to write the last entry, explaining why Cromwell turned down the crown.

   Read the diary entries and then, in rough:

   a) Jot down words that describe how Cromwell felt about taking this decision: for example, easy, difficult, worrying. Think about how long it took him to make this decision.

   b) Make a list of the possible reasons why Cromwell turned down the crown.

   c) Decide which of these reasons was the most important – or do you think his decision was based on a mixture of reasons?

   d) Now write Cromwell's diary entry for 8 May 1657, the day he turned down the crown.

2 As you work through Unit 1.4, fill in your Hero or Villain scales with the evidence you find.

31 March 1657

Parliament has offered me the crown. I asked for time to make my answer. This is the weightiest, hardest thing that has ever been asked of any man. I must ask advice of God and of my own heart.

8 April 1657

Again I have asked MPs for more time. I have great difficulties in my mind over this decision.

12 April 1657

I had arranged to meet MPs to discuss the offer but cancelled the meeting because of poor health. Anxiety over this decision is making me ill. It will be a disaster for our country if I go against God's will in this decision. But what is God's will?

13 April 1657

I am almost completely decided against the crown. Truly, God has laid aside this title of king. It has been the issue of a long civil war when much blood was shed. God struck not only at the person of the king but also the title. I will not try to set up something God has destroyed and laid in the dust.

21 April 1657

The greatest difficulties remain in my mind. The Hand of God was with us at Marston Moor and at Naseby. Does God now want me to take the crown so that I can better defend the church against its enemies?

5 May 1657

I remain uncertain but am coming to the view that it would be better to accept the crown. The people want a king again and it will end the uncertainty of what will happen after my death. If I am king, then my son will take the crown in his turn ...

Later. Generals Fleetwood and Desborough came to dinner. I tried out on them the idea of accepting the crown. I did not do it directly but joked that taking the crown was no more important than a man putting a feather in his cap. They replied that it was truly important and that I would ruin both myself and my friends if I became king.

6 May 1657

I have decided to accept the crown, despite the Generals. I shall tell the family this evening. They will be the first to know. Now that I have made my mind up I feel that God has taken a great weight off my mind.

Later. Walking in the park I met Generals Fleetwood, Lambert and Desborough. They told me very strongly once again that they and the army are strongly against me becoming king. They are the men I fought alongside for so many years. I am in torment again ...

7 May 1657

Arranged to meet the MPs at 11 a.m., then put them off until later. In the evening I went to the stables to look at my new horse and found the MPs still waiting! I shall give them my decision tomorrow. What does God want me to do?

ACTIVITY

◆ Interpretations of Cromwell

Even during his lifetime, Cromwell was very controversial. People argued fiercely about whether he was a good or a bad man, especially when he was offered the crown. Sources 1 and 2 show you two artists' interpretations of Cromwell. Work in pairs. One of you should study Source 1, the other should study Source 2.

1 In Source 1 can you find:

- ◆ the crown
- ◆ the sword of justice
- ◆ the orb, symbol of a king's power
- ◆ royal robes
- ◆ armour
- ◆ devils
- ◆ Charles' execution?

2 Do you think the artist in Source 1 wanted Cromwell to be king?

3 In Source 2 can you find:

- ◆ a Bible
- ◆ Greek words (they mean 'I worship only God')
- ◆ two pillars (symbols of power)
- ◆ a dove holding an olive branch (symbols of peace)
- ◆ Noah's Ark being guided by God from a flood to safety on top of a mountain
- ◆ the people of England, Scotland and Ireland offering gifts to Cromwell
- ◆ false religions being trampled underneath Cromwell's feet
- ◆ people living peaceful and wealthy lives?

4 Do you think the artist in Source 2 wanted Cromwell to be king?

5 Explain to your partner what your artist was trying to say about Cromwell in his picture.

6 Which interpretation of Cromwell do you think is right and why?

WITHAL

SOURCE 1 A cartoon of Cromwell drawn by a Dutch artist *c.* 1649.

SOURCE 2 A drawing of Cromwell by an English artist, 1658.

THE MAN WHO HATED CHRISTMAS?

Find out whether Cromwell really hated people having fun

Some people believe that Cromwell was a killjoy, who hated people having fun, and a religious BIGOT, who punished people who held different beliefs from him. Does the evidence support this view? These Cromwell Close-ups will help you decide.

A C T I V I T Y

1 Cromwell's enemies said that Cromwell was a killjoy and religious bigot. Which Close-ups could be used to support this view?
2 Cromwell's supporters disagreed. They said he liked to enjoy himself and was tolerant of other religions. Which Close-ups could be used to support their view?
3 Can any of the Close-ups be used to support both views?
4 Who do you think was right about Cromwell – his enemies or his supporters?
5 Which of Cromwell's actions are most important for deciding what kind of man he was?

CROMWELL CLOSE-UPS

1 Cromwell was a caring father and husband. He was happily married for 38 years. He had eight children. Three of his children died before him. Each time he was devastated.

2 Puritans like Oliver Cromwell believed that God had given them victory in the Civil War. So they had a duty to make people in England more godly by making Sunday a holy day and stopping drunkenness, swearing and gambling.

3 In 1642 Cromwell supported MPs when they voted to close all theatres in London. Puritans thought that theatres were evil places.

4 At his daughter Frances' wedding in 1657, Cromwell played practical jokes on the women. He threw a sticky drink over their dresses and put wet sweets on their chairs.

5 As Lord Protector, Cromwell let Catholics worship in private, as long as they did not cause any trouble.

6 On his way to fight a battle against the Scots, Cromwell stopped to laugh at some soldiers playing with a cream tub. One was sticking it over the head of another.

7 Cromwell loved music and singing. As Lord Protector, he employed an organist and a violinist. He also held dances in his official residence.

8 Puritans like Cromwell believed that church worship should be based only on what the Bible said. So Cromwell believed that there should be no music or singing during church services. He also believed that statues, paintings and stained-glass windows had no place in churches.

9 As Lord Protector, Cromwell was worried that enemies plotted against the government at sports events, and in ale houses.

10 In 1644 Cromwell supported MPs when they voted for a law to make everyone observe Sunday as the Lord's Day.

11 In 1647 Parliament voted to ban Christmas and Easter – because they were not mentioned in the Bible and were associated with the Catholic Church. Cromwell agreed with this. New holidays once a month were introduced to replace Christmas and Easter.

12 In 1650 Cromwell strongly supported Parliament when it introduced religious toleration – allowing all Protestants (but NOT Catholics) to worship in their own way.

13 In 1655, after a Royalist rebellion, Lord Protector Cromwell divided the country into eleven districts and appointed a Major General to control each one. He told them to:

◆ stop 'horse races, cock fighting, bear baitings, plays, or any unlawful assemblies . . . because treason and rebellion is usually contrived upon such occasions, and much evil and wickedness committed'

◆ stop people swearing and getting drunk

◆ help to look after poor people

◆ close all alehouses and taverns in remote parts of the country.

14 Cromwell loved horse-racing, hawking and hunting, and other sports. In 1654 he watched a hurling match (a form of hockey) in Hyde Park followed by a display of wrestling.

15 Jews had been expelled from England during the Middle Ages. Cromwell allowed Jews back into England for the first time in 400 years although his advisers and MPs said this was wrong.

16 Cromwell liked to relax by smoking tobacco and drinking a glass of wine.

17 In 1656 a QUAKER called James Nayler rode on a donkey into Bristol, dressed like Jesus. MPs found him guilty of BLASPHEMY – they had him whipped, branded and put in prison for life. Cromwell did not like Nayler's behaviour but he told MPs they had no right to punish him like this for it.

ACTIVITY

Use these Close-ups to add more evidence to your Hero or Villain scales.

Oliver Cromwell died on 3 September 1658. He was 59. He was given a hero's funeral and buried in Westminster Abbey just like a king. Since then, peoples' views have changed!

ACTIVITY

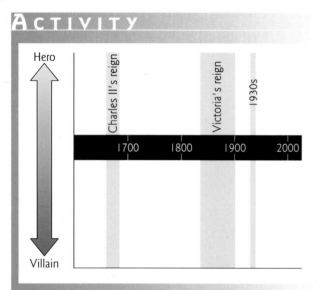

Your task is to make a graph to show how and why ideas about Cromwell have changed since his death.

1 Your teacher may give you a larger copy of this graph.

2 Using the information on these two pages, draw either a thumbs up (hero) or a thumbs down (villain) on each period to show whether Cromwell was seen as a hero or a villain.

3 Around each thumb make brief notes to explain *why* people at that time had that idea about Cromwell.

How have historians viewed Cromwell?

CHARLES II's REIGN (1660–85)

People thought Cromwell was a monster who killed Charles I to seize power for himself.

In 1661 they dug up his decaying body (see page 1), beheaded it and threw the body in a ditch. They displayed the skull on a spike outside Parliament (Source 1).

VICTORIAN PERIOD (1837–1901)

People thought Cromwell was a great man who had helped to make Britain a fairer, stronger and more religious country.

In 1899 they put a statue of Cromwell, holding a Bible and a sword, right outside the Houses of Parliament (Source 2)

It wasn't just historians who knew about Cromwell. In Yorkshire, people talking about times when ordinary people were well-off still said it was just like in 'Oliver's days'.

THE 1930s AND 1940s

Many historians thought that Cromwell was a cruel military dictator.

. . . TODAY

Most historians see Cromwell as a puzzling and complicated man:

• an MP who believed in parliamentary government AND a soldier who believed that the army did the work of God

• a revolutionary who supported the execution of Charles I AND a conservative who wanted to protect the power of landowners

• a deeply religious man AND one who was often tortured by doubt as he struggled to discover God's will for him and for the country

• a ruler who made mistakes but had many successes and who always wanted the best for his country.

Why have they viewed Cromwell this way?

Changes made during Cromwell's rule were reversed. Music, dancing, horse-racing and gambling were allowed. Theatres reopened. Colourful clothes came back into fashion. Puritans were punished.

People blamed Cromwell for all the troubles of the past. Historians made up stories to show Cromwell as a villain. One told how the four-year-old Cromwell had punched two-year-old Prince Charles and made his nose bleed. This story cannot be true. Young Prince Charles and young Cromwell never met.

- The Victorians were proud of being ruled by an elected Parliament.
- They admired the soldiers who had built up their empire.
- Most middle-class people were Protestants but everyone could worship freely.
- Middle-class Victorians disapproved of drinking and gambling.

The Victorians said that Cromwell helped make Britain like this. He had helped to:
- create a parliamentary system of government
- start the British Empire
- establish religious freedom
- improve the moral behaviour of the people.

In 1845 Cromwell's letters and speeches were published for the first time. Now people could study Cromwell's own words rather than what his enemies wrote about him.

Several countries in Europe were ruled by dictators. Hitler had risen from a humble background to become leader of Germany. Hitler hated elected governments. He believed that his country needed a strong leader. He won support from the army, and banned elections and other political parties. He ended religious freedom and controlled newspapers, film and radio. Millions of opponents and Jews were imprisoned or murdered. Hitler's invasions of other countries led to the Second World War (1939–45).

Historians try to judge Oliver Cromwell by the standards of his own time rather than our own. They try to reach balanced conclusions about his strengths and weaknesses, successes and failures.

However, people still argue about Cromwell.

There is an internet site run by the Cromwell Association if you want to find out more about him: www.cromwell.argonet.co.uk

SOURCE 1 Cromwell's skull. It is now owned by Cambridge University.

SOURCE 2 Cromwell's statue outside the Houses of Parliament. It was erected in 1899 to mark the 300th anniversary of his birth. There were fierce protests from Irish MPs and the House of Lords.

◆ *Was Cromwell important in history?*

When we say that someone is important in history, it does not just mean that someone is famous. It means more than that. On the right are five CRITERIA why someone could be important in history.

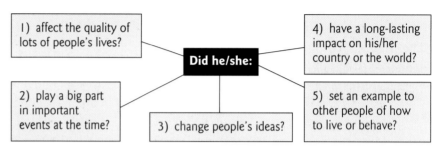

1) affect the quality of lots of people's lives?

Did he/she:

4) have a long-lasting impact on his/her country or the world?

2) play a big part in important events at the time?

3) change people's ideas?

5) set an example to other people of how to live or behave?

ACTIVITY A:
HOW IMPORTANT WAS CROMWELL?

1 How does Cromwell measure up against the five criteria? Use the work you have done so far in Section 1 to complete your own copy of this table.
2 Below are some reasons why many historians think Cromwell was important in history. Which one do you think is the most important reason? Explain why you have chosen that reason. You can add a reason of your own if you think it is very important.
   a) He played a very important part in winning the Civil War for Parliament.
   b) He was a good man who always tried to follow his beliefs.
   c) He helped to make Parliament more important than the monarchy.
   d) He came from an ordinary background to be ruler of Britain.
   e) He gave British people greater religious freedom than ever before.

Did Cromwell:	Score 1–10	Evidence
1) affect the quality of lots of people's lives?		
2) play a big part in important events at the time?		
3) change people's ideas?		
4) have a long-lasting impact on his country or the world?		
5) set an example to other people of how to live or behave?		

ACTIVITY B:
WHO IS MOST IMPORTANT?

1 Choose an example of someone from the past or today who is famous but not important in history and explain why.
2 Now think about the five criteria in the spider diagram above. Choose the three people you think are most important from page 47 and complete your own copy of this table.
3 Who else do you think deserves to be known as important in history and why? Add them to your table.

Name	Criteria why this person is important in history (use the numbers 1–5)	Explain your choice (what did this person do that matches these criteria?)

William the Conqueror:
the Middle Ages
Won the battle of Hastings in
1066 and established Norman
rule in England.

King John: the Middle Ages
Signed Magna Carta with the
barons in 1215.

Elizabeth I: 16th century
Queen of England in 1588
when the Spanish Armada
was beaten, and who tried to
stop religious hatred.

William Shakespeare: late
15th/early 16th century
The author of over 30 plays.
They are still performed all
over the world.

Michael Faraday:
19th century
The scientist who discovered
how to use electricity in 1831.

Louis Pasteur: 19th century
The scientist whose discovery
of germs in the 1850s led to
the first effective cures for
diseases.

Emmeline Pankhurst:
early 20th century
Led the suffragette campaigns
for 'Votes for Women'.

Alan Turing: 20th century
The mathematical genius
whose work in the 1930s led
to the development of
computers.

Winston Churchill:
20th century
Prime Minister who inspired
Britain to victory over Hitler
during the Second World
War (1939–45).

Mahatma Gandhi:
20th century
Led peaceful campaigns for
civil rights in South Africa and
in India for independence
from the British Empire.

John Lennon:
20th century
Musician whose records have
been played all over the world
since the 1960s.

David Beckham:
late 20th/early 21st century
Famous footballer and captain
of the England team during
the 2002 World Cup.

By now you have gathered lots of evidence about Cromwell. It is time for your BIG FINISH! The next seven pages will help you to write a biography of Cromwell that you can be really proud of . . .

On pages 50–54 we will help you to plan and write your biography, but first here is some advice from successful historical biographers.

ACTIVITY

1 Read Sources 1–5. Try to find examples of how Antonia Fraser:
   a) uses interesting analogies (comparisons with familiar situations) to help explain something
   b) creates an atmosphere of drama and suspense to grab the reader's attention
   c) explains different possibilities when she is not certain about something
   d) uses interesting details to help the reader imagine the situation
   e) refers to the sources she has studied.
2 Who do you think she is writing for? How do you know?
3 What does she think of Cromwell? How do you know?
4 What kinds of different sources might she have used to find out her facts?
5 Which of the five extracts do you like the best? Why?

---

1 **First decide who you are writing for.** A book for young people is different from a book for adults.

2 **Make it exciting.** Cromwell's life was full of exciting events and dramatic decisions. Make sure that readers will want to keep turning the pages!

3 **Don't make things up.** Think like a historian. Use evidence from the time. If you sometimes *have* to guess or use your imagination, be honest enough to tell your readers that is what you are doing. Say things like 'I don't know what happened next, but it is possible to imagine what might have flashed across Cromwell's mind at that moment . . . ' This is called speculation and biographers do it a lot.

4 **Cut out unnecessary detail.** You will bore your readers if you write everything you know about Cromwell! Focus on the key events and decisions.

5 **Remember things were different then.** Judge people by the standards of their own time, not by our standards today. For example, perhaps religion isn't important to you but in the 1600s religion was a vital part of Cromwell's life and is essential in explaining his actions.

6 **Include well-known stories, but say if they are true or false.**

7 **Get inside his skin.** A good biography is not just a list of things someone did. It would be very boring if it just said: 'First Cromwell did this, then he did that.' A good biography helps readers 'get to know' the person, to get inside his or her thoughts.

8 **Be balanced.** Your biography needs to show Cromwell's successes *and* failures, his good points and his weaknesses. Cromwell would like that. Remember, you found out that he told an artist who painted his portrait: 'Paint my picture exactly like me and do not flatter me at all. Show all these wrinkles, pimples, warts and everything as you see me.' (See page 4.)

Antonia Fraser is a very successful biographer. In 1973 she wrote one of the most famous biographies of Oliver Cromwell, called *Cromwell, Our Chief of Men*. Sources 1–5 are extracts from it.

Antonia Fraser

SOURCE 1 Here she describes Oliver as he was about to make his first important speech in Parliament in 1640.

He was very ordinarily dressed in a plain cloth suit, which appeared to have been made by a bad country tailor. It was plain, and not very clean; and there was even a speck or two of blood on his neckband. The general carelessness of his outfit was completed by the fact that the hat was without a hatband.

SOURCE 2 Cromwell travelling to Ireland, 1649.

The Irish Sea was choppy, the crossing was uncomfortable and Cromwell turned out not to be a good sailor. Before he even left the harbour, according to Hugh Peter who accompanied him, Cromwell was as seasick as ever he had seen a man in his life.

SOURCE 3 Cromwell opening his first Parliament as Lord Protector in September 1654.

In the manner of a headmaster who assures his school that each pupil is as important to the structure as himself, Cromwell spoke kindly to Parliament on the subject of its future task, and added 'I shall exercise plainness and freeness with you, in telling you that I have not spoken these things as one that assumes to himself dominion [power] over you, but as one that doth resolve to be a fellow servant with you . . .'

SOURCE 4 Cromwell deciding whether to accept the crown, in 1657.

The Protector's unreliable health began to play a part in the proceedings, and several planned meetings with MPs had to be cancelled at the last minute. Whether it was indeed ill health or whether the agonies of indecision were the cause of his illness, the whole atmosphere was fraught with tension. And when the Protector did meet MPs again on 20 April they found him half dressed, in his gown, with a black scarf tied around his neck. The long drawn out drama of it all held everyone in London and indeed far abroad enthralled. The day to day letters of those involved, reporting the twists and turns of the Protector's mood, began to take on the quality of a thrilling if agonising story of suspense.

SOURCE 5 Describing the 'execution' of Cromwell in 1661.

About ten o'clock, still in their grave clothes – Cromwell and Ireton were in green cloth, Bradshaw in white – they were hung up in full gaze of the public, at angles to each other. Bradshaw occupied the central position. At four o'clock, the corpses were taken down. The common hangman proceeded to hack off the heads. In the heavy muffling of the grave clothes round the neck, it took eight blows to get off Cromwell's head, six to chop off that of Ireton. It seems that fingers and toes were hacked off at the same time, and Cromwell's skull may have lost an eye. The three headless bodies were put into a deep pit dug beneath the gallows. But the heads were taken to Westminster Hall and five days later stuck up outside on poles of oak tipped with iron.

◆ *Writing your biography*

Before you start

There are many different ways you could write your biography. These suggestions are to help you to focus on the important parts of Cromwell's story. You don't have to use them if you have better ideas. Like any book, your biography should be divided into chapters. They do not have to be long or even of the same length. Some chapters might need only two paragraphs. Make sure that your writing for each chapter is clear and interesting, using words from your Cromwell word bank. Remember to support your conclusions with evidence. Try to make the end of one chapter flow naturally into the next. Think of an interesting title for each chapter that will make people want to read it. Refer to the evidence you have collected in the scales throughout Section 1.

CHAPTER 1 **The Test of Strength**

(Page 51)

Now you can launch into your story.

You could start with Cromwell's childhood – or jump straight to 1640 and Cromwell arriving at Parliament. You want to make your readers understand why Cromwell was angry with the King.

> **Key tip:**
> Focus on religion. Religion was Cromwell's driving force.

Fast forward to 1642 and write another paragraph(s) about the start of the war. Explain that no one knows for sure when or why Cromwell decided to fight, but speculate about why he decided. Explain why this was such a big decision for Cromwell – to fight against God's appointed ruler. Then give some hard evidence that shows how determined he was to fight once he had made the decision.

INTRODUCTION **The Hall of Mirrors**

(Page 50)

It's nearly always best to write your introduction last so come back to this at the end.

But before you set off, it *is* important that you reach one overall decision. Do you think Cromwell was a hero, a villain or a mixture? Note down your view and a couple of your main reasons why.

> **Key tip:**
> As you write, don't chop and change your opinion about Cromwell. Be consistent about whether he was a hero or a villain.

CHAPTER 2 **The Dodgems**

(Page 51)

This could be an exciting blood and glory section! You could choose just one battle (such as Marston Moor) and describe Cromwell's role in it. Say what made him successful. Was it because he was brave? Clever? A good leader? Chose good soldiers? Or was it God who gave him victory?

You could choose to be more *analytical*. Give Cromwell a mark out of ten for importance (ten out of ten means he won the war single-handed!), then explain your score. Be sure to say whether Cromwell would have agreed with your score.

> **Key tip:**
> Back up your opinions with evidence from pages 18–27.

CHAPTER 3 The Ghost Train

(Page 51)

Choose at least one incident out of three in the book: the execution of Charles I, the shooting of the Levellers, or the massacre of the Irish Catholics. Make the story as interesting as possible. Make sure you explain why Cromwell made the decisions he did. Was he just a cruel man who killed those who got in his way? Or was he doing the best he could for his country and his religion?

> **Key tip:**
> You should be able to reuse some of your work from the tasks on pages 28–37.

CHAPTER 4 Hoopla!

(Page 50)

This was Cromwell's greatest and most difficult decision. We know he decided against being king – you need to explain why. This can be a short chapter.

> **Key tip:**
> Use the diary extracts from pages 38–39.

CHAPTER 5 Father Christmas's Grotto

(Page 50)

So far you have been writing about wars, politics and difficult decisions. This is your chance to describe Cromwell's personality. What was he really like? Friendly, likeable, good company? Or a miserable killjoy who hated other people enjoying themselves? And if he was a bit of both, which was the stronger?

> **Key tip:**
> Don't just state your opinion. Include evidence about Cromwell to support it.

CHAPTER 6 The Fortune Teller

(Page 50)

Over the centuries, people have changed their minds about Cromwell. First he was a villain, then a hero, then a villain again. Can you explain why? This is a tricky one. It's not really part of Cromwell's life story so you could leave it out – but if you write some good paragraphs here it will show you understand a lot about history!

CONCLUSION...

Finish by giving your opinion about Cromwell. Was he a hero or villain? Why is he a very important person in British history?

> **Key tip:**
> Mention your two most important pieces of evidence again.

... then back to your Introduction

Professional authors find it is usually best to write introductions last!

What will you put in your Introduction? It needs to explain the two views of Cromwell and to sum up what your biography will cover, but it also needs to grab your readers' attention – so they will want to keep reading! Have a look at a couple of other biographies and decide if you like the way they start. You could start with a really dramatic moment such as the 'execution' of Cromwell's corpse; or a quote by Cromwell himself. Make your readers interested in reading your book!

> Turn to the next page for our final tips.

Almost finished – revising and editing

Revise and check each chapter so that it is work you can be proud of. Don't miss out this stage. Check everything carefully. Improve pieces that you are not happy with.

Top tips for revising and editing

Creative checks:
1. Do you think the writing is interesting/enjoyable?
2. Is everything clear and accurate?
3. Have you supported your arguments with evidence?
4. Have you made clear whether you think Cromwell was a hero or villain – or a mixture of both?
5. Check your writing against the suggestions on page 48.

Technical checks:
6. Use a dictionary to check spellings that you are not sure of.
7. Use a full stop at the end of every sentence.
8. Use capital letters for names and to start every new sentence.
9. Use paragraphs. Is it clear where each paragraph starts and ends?
10. Check the length of your sentences. Put in some short, sharp sentences. It adds variety and interest.

Finishing touches! Turning your work into a book

1. Choose the size of your pages. Try A5 to be different.
2. Decide on a title for your book. Keep it short and snappy. Include Cromwell's name with a short phrase or question to make people interested in reading about him.
3. Choose a title for each of your chapters. Use a short phrase or question that sums up what the chapter is about. Use bigger print for the chapter titles than the main text.
4. Decide whether to include your timeline in your book.
5. Choose **TWO** pictures to go in your book and decide where they should go. You could use pictures from this book or find other pictures of Cromwell from a CD-ROM or the internet – there are lots of pictures at www.cromwell.argonet.co.uk. Make sure that you write a caption for each picture.
6. Make a contents page. It should be the first page in your book. It should contain the titles of each chapter and the numbers of the pages on which they begin.
7. Design your cover. It should be in colour and contain the title of the book, the author's name (that's you!) and a picture of Cromwell. Make your cover as eye-catching as possible. Try to choose a picture, or draw your own, that fits with your title. For example, if it is *Cromwell the Villain*, use a picture that makes him look like a villain.

Now print out your work. Put it in a folder or staple the pages together. Your biography is complete!

CONGRATULATIONS!

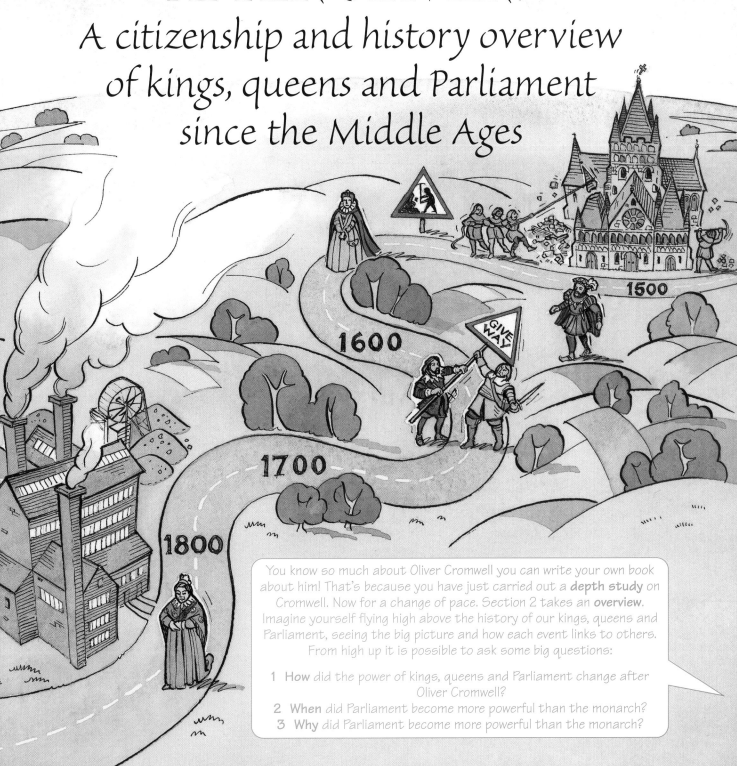

WHAT HAPPENED AFTER OLIVER?

A citizenship and history overview
of kings, queens and Parliament
since the Middle Ages

1500

1600

1700

1800

You know so much about Oliver Cromwell you can write your own book
about him! That's because you have just carried out a **depth study** on
Cromwell. Now for a change of pace. Section 2 takes an **overview**.
Imagine yourself flying high above the history of our kings, queens and
Parliament, seeing the big picture and how each event links to others.
From high up it is possible to ask some big questions:

1 **How** did the power of kings, queens and Parliament change after
Oliver Cromwell?

2 **When** did Parliament become more powerful than the monarch?

3 **Why** did Parliament become more powerful than the monarch?

WHEN DID PARLIAMENT TAKE OVER THE MONARCH'S POWER?

"We executed Charles I, but they brought back Charles II to be king after my death. So when did Parliament finally take over power from the kings and queens? If you play this game, you'll get some clues here and then you can see if your answers are right on pages 58–59."

ACTIVITY

a) Get into groups of three. You will each need a marker or counter to move round the board.

b) Each of you choose one of the first three kings below and place your counter on his starting square.

c) Take turns to move one square each, following the instructions in the squares. As you go, add up the points the monarchy scores.

d) Keep a note of the final scores and then repeat the game with the other three kings.

e) Look at the totals for the six kings. If the monarchy has ten points or more then it has more power than Parliament. If it has less than ten then Parliament has more power. When did Parliament become more powerful than the monarch?

Charles II (1660–85)
Your father, Charles I, was executed but now you have been invited back to be king. Start at square 17.

James II (1685–88)
You follow your brother, Charles, as king. You too can remember why your father was executed. Start at square 13.

William III (1689–1702)
You rule Holland but you have been invited to rule England with your wife, Mary, the daughter of the last king, James II. Start at square 23.

George I (1714–27)
You rule Hanover in Germany but you have been invited to rule England because you are the nearest Protestant relative of the last monarch, Queen Anne. Start at square 21.

George III (1760–1820)
You inherit the throne from your father, George II. Start at square 11.

George IV (1820–30)
You have been REGENT for ten years during your father's illness. Now you can be king yourself – or have you lost all your power? Start at square 14.

When did Parliament take over the monarch's power?

1 You agree to new rules that monarchs have to obey. You have to ask Parliament for permission before you can leave the country or declare war. Score 1 point. Now add up William III's score.

2 You have lost your empire in America. It is a disaster. You want to keep fighting but in the end you have to give in. Gain 1 point. Go to square 24.

3 You do not have enough support to fight and you remember the horrors of the Civil War. You give in and flee abroad. Gain 0 points. Now add up James II's score.

4 A new law! You must call Parliament every three years. In fact, Parliament meets every year because of all your wars and so is becoming more powerful. Score 2 points. Go to square 1.

5 You try to stop the Prime Minister giving jobs to people you do not like – but you cannot stop him. Score 0 points. Go to square 12 – if you dare!

6 People have stopped thinking that the King is chosen by God so they have stopped expecting you to cure them of diseases just by touching them. Score 0 points. Now add up George I's score.

7 You do not *have* to call Parliament but you do, because you need Parliament for money. Score 3 points. Go to square 9 for some bad news.

8 James Stuart (son of James II) invades Scotland, hoping to take your crown. You beat him easily. Score 5 points. Go to square 20. You are doing well so far.

9 At heart you are a Catholic but you dare not change the religion back to Catholicism or Parliament will get rid of you, just like your father. Score 0 points. Now add up Charles II's score.

10 By 1688 there are rumours that you will make the whole country Catholic. Parliament invites your daughter, Mary, and her husband, William, to replace you. You have gone too far! Gain 1 point. Go to square 3.

11 At first you are able to stop politicians you dislike from becoming Prime Minister – but not always! Gain 4 points. Go to square 2 and get ready to cry.

12 It is 1827. The Prime Minister is ill. You need to choose the next Prime Minister but you dither. Then you ask the other ministers to choose. You seem to have no power at all! Score 0 points. Now add up George IV's score.

13 You begin by calling Parliament. Although you are Catholic, MPs seem happy that you are King. You have the same powers as your brother before you. Score 5 points. Go to square 22.

14 You take over as Regent when your father becomes ill but you have no real power. The Prime Minister is running the war with France. Gain 1 point. Go to square 19.

15 You can still choose your own advisers and decide if the country goes to war – but you need Parliament to give you taxes to pay for those wars. Score 4 points. Go to square 7.

16 Pitt wants to give Catholics the vote but you make him resign as Prime Minister because you disagree. Then, you have to let him return! Gain 2 points. Now add up George III's score.

17 Great start! The people want a king again! Thousands expect you to cure them of a skin disease called the King's Evil – just by touching them! Score 5 points. Go to square 15.

18 The good news – you decide on your advisers. The bad news – you need Parliament to give you money for war. You cannot reject laws made by Parliament. Score 3 points. Go to square 4.

19 You want to end your marriage to Princess Caroline and you ask the Prime Minister to arrange it. However, Parliament does not agree and so you have to stay married. Score 0 points. Go to square 5.

20 Someone has to run the country when you go back to Hanover. Robert Walpole becomes the first Prime Minister but you choose your advisers and declare war. Score 3 points. Go to square 6.

21 Parliament chose you as king because you are Protestant. Over 50 other people have a better claim to the crown but they are all Catholics. Gain 2 points. Go to square 8 to see if any of them challenge you.

22 You decide to promote Catholics in the army and navy and as judges. You have the power to do this and at first there is no trouble. Gain 4 points. Go to square 10.

23 You were chosen as king by Parliament. Parliament helps you fight wars against France throughout your reign – and you win! Score 4 points. Go to square 18.

24 Despite defeat in America nobody wants to rebel. You are powerful enough to help William Pitt stay as Prime Minister although he is only 24 and has many enemies. Gain 2 points. Go to square 16.

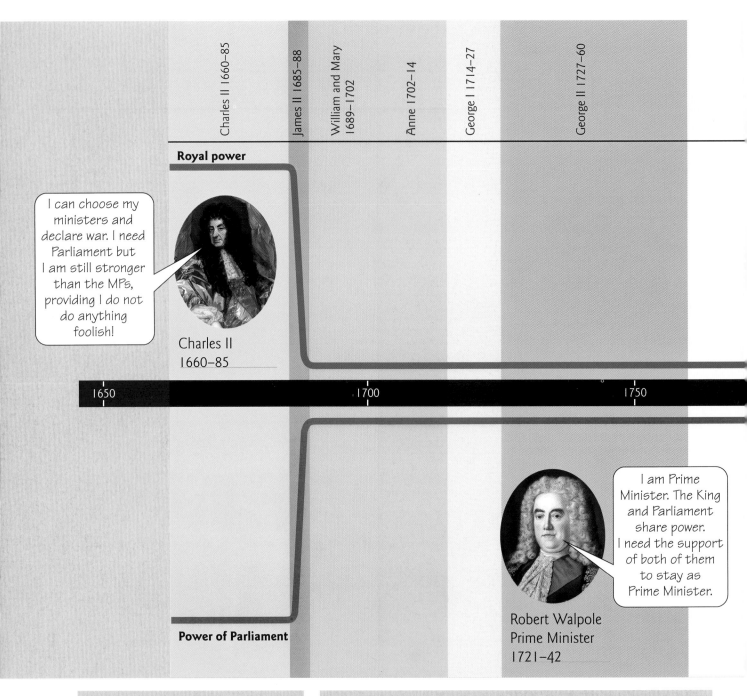

Charles II 1660–85

James II 1685–88

William and Mary 1689–1702

Anne 1702–14

George I 1714–27

George II 1727–60

Royal power

I can choose my ministers and declare war. I need Parliament but I am still stronger than the MPs, providing I do not do anything foolish!

Charles II
1660–85

1650 1700 1750

I am Prime Minister. The King and Parliament share power. I need the support of both of them to stay as Prime Minister.

Power of Parliament

Robert Walpole
Prime Minister
1721–42

Stage 1: 1660–88

Charles II kept most of his power by staying on good terms with Parliament. He did not make changes that Parliament did not want. However, his brother, James II, did not learn from Charles. James was a strong Catholic. MPs thought that James was trying to rule without Parliament and make the whole country change from Protestant to Catholic, so they DEPOSED him. James fled abroad without fighting. Now Parliament had the chance to choose the new monarchs, Mary, James II's daughter and her husband, William of Orange. Parliament's power increased.

Stage 2: 1688–1780s

After 1688 the monarch and Parliament shared power. The most important change was the appointment of a Prime Minister. The Prime Minister needed the support of both the monarch and Parliament to keep his job. He could not stay as Prime Minister just because the monarch wanted him.

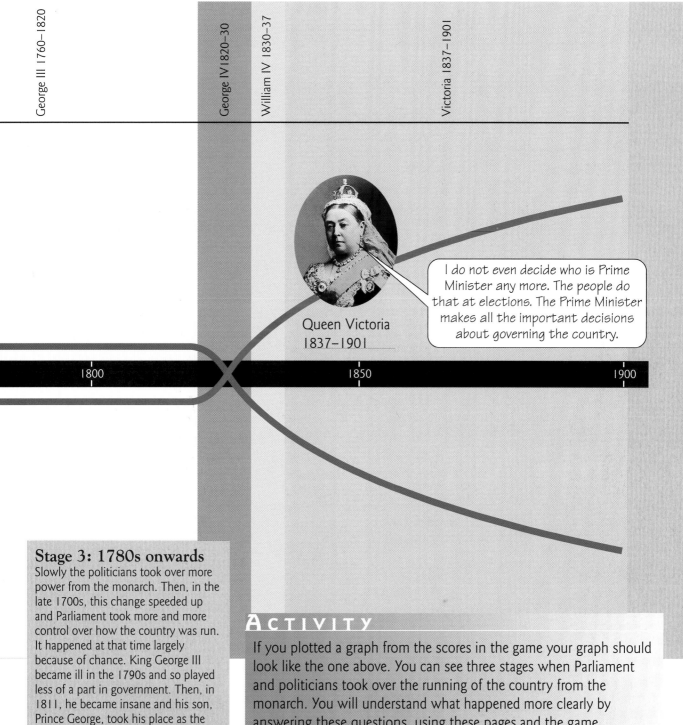

George III 1760–1820

George IV 1820–30

William IV 1830–37

Victoria 1837–1901

Queen Victoria
1837–1901

I do not even decide who is Prime Minister any more. The people do that at elections. The Prime Minister makes all the important decisions about governing the country.

1800

1850

1900

Stage 3: 1780s onwards

Slowly the politicians took over more power from the monarch. Then, in the late 1700s, this change speeded up and Parliament took more and more control over how the country was run. It happened at that time largely because of chance. King George III became ill in the 1790s and so played less of a part in government. Then, in 1811, he became insane and his son, Prince George, took his place as the Regent. Prince George was not clever enough to take part in government and he was not interested either. When he became King himself he was happy to let the politicians decide the things that previous kings had always insisted on doing themselves. In 1827 he even let the politicians choose the new Prime Minister. George IV gave away the power that earlier kings and queens had fought so hard to keep!

ACTIVITY

If you plotted a graph from the scores in the game your graph should look like the one above. You can see three stages when Parliament and politicians took over the running of the country from the monarch. You will understand what happened more clearly by answering these questions, using these pages and the game.

1 What had Charles II learned from his father?
2 Why was James II deposed?
3 Why was the first Prime Minister appointed?
4 Write out the following sentences and explain what evidence you would use to prove that they are true:
   a) The monarch and Parliament shared power after 1688.
   b) By 1827 Parliament and politicians were more powerful than the monarch.

"The game helped you to work out WHEN Parliament became more powerful than the monarch. Now you need to work out WHY Parliament became so powerful."

ACTIVITY

The picture below shows you the reasons why Parliament became more powerful than the monarch. When you have had a good look at it, look at the opposite page. Which reasons do you think should get the gold, silver and bronze medals? Give the gold to the most important reason why Parliament became more powerful than the monarch – and so on. Or was it a dead heat?

The full story – monarchy and Parliament since 1066

Royal
power

| 1066 | 1215 | 1280s |

1066
Norman
Conquest

1215
Magna Carta – the barons
forced King John to agree
rules about how he ran the
country but John broke the
agreement.

1272–1307
Edward I was the first king to call frequent
Parliaments because he needed money for
his wars in Wales, Scotland and France.
Even then, Parliament only met for a few
weeks and ended when the King told it to
end. There was often no Parliament for four
or five years.

Monarchy and Parliament to 1500

The power of the monarchy stayed high in
the Middle Ages. This was because people
believed that kings were chosen by God and
that there was no alternative to monarchy.

Kings were also needed as leaders in war.
All good kings led their armies in battle.
Parliament was only called when the
King needed money for war.

1530s
Henry VIII used Parliament to pass laws creating the Church of England and make him Head of the Church. This increased the monarchy's power in the short term but also gave some people a reason to rebel if they disagreed with the monarch's religion. Henry's religious laws also made Parliament more important.

ACTIVITY

1 Which event do you think was the most important turning point in the history of the monarchy? Explain your choice.
2 What part does the monarch play in government today?

1530s

1642–49
Civil War – Parliament went to war with Charles I because he tried to rule without the help and agreement of Parliament. Charles was executed in 1649.

1642–49

1688

1688
James II was deposed by Parliament because people thought he was going to force everyone to become Catholic. The new King and Queen were Protestants chosen by Parliament.

Monarchy and Parliament after 1500

After Henry VIII's reign, there was more than one religion. Some people thought it was more important to be loyal to their religion than to the monarch. This led to civil war in the 1640s.

The power of the monarchy began to get weaker in the 1600s. Monarch and Parliament shared power after 1688 but Parliament became much more powerful than the monarchy between 1790 and 1830.

In the 1700s the Prime Minister became an alternative leader and government also became more complicated as towns grew and the population increased. It was important not to depend on one person to rule the country. Kings no longer led their armies into battle.

1720s
Robert Walpole became the first Prime Minister. Now monarch and Parliament shared power between them. A monarch could still stop a politician becoming Prime Minister if he or she did not like him.

1720s

1820–30
Parliament had become far more powerful than the monarch by the time of George IV.

Late 1800s
Gladstone became Prime Minister four times, even though Queen Victoria did not like him.

COMPLICATED SOCIETY / THE ALTERNATIVE / RELIGION / WAR

What about us – the ordinary people? We Levellers wanted every man to have the vote but you haven't said what happened about that. Parliament may have got more power than the King by 1800 but Parliament was still full of lords and rich landowners. I want to know when ordinary people got the vote and a say in government. Don't forget we died for the vote!

63

We began by asking you whether Cromwell was a hero or a villain but you have learned about a lot more than just the life story of Cromwell. You have studied wars, religion, pastimes and a whole sweep of kings. The next activity gives you the chance to applaud your own knowledge. How many of the questions below do you know the answer to? Don't worry – you don't have to answer them again. It's your chance to realise just how much you have learned. There are some questions here that you can't answer yet – but you will, once you have studied later periods of history.

ACTIVITY A

Look at the picture.

1 Which questions can you answer after working on this book?
2 Which questions remain unanswered?

THE KNOWLEDGE FILES

Why is Cromwell such an important person in British history?

When did Parliament become more powerful than the monarchy?

What kinds of soldiers and weapons did they have in the Civil War?

Why was Charles I executed?

How did ordinary people win the vote?

Why did Parliament become more powerful than the monarchy?

When did all adult men and women get the chance to vote?

Why was religion so important in the sixteenth and seventeenth centuries?

Did the Civil War destroy the power of the monarchy for ever?

Who started the Church of England?

Why did the Civil War begin?

Did ordinary people have a say in government in the sixteenth and seventeenth centuries?

Why have interpretations of Cromwell changed since the seventeenth century?

Was Christmas ever abolished?

ACTIVITY B

The Activities in this book have also been designed to improve your historical skills. Look carefully at the **History Skills Wall**.

1 Which skills have you improved through studying this book?
2 Which skills do you need to develop further?
3 Before your next unit of work in history, design an action plan for yourself. Set yourself three targets – skills that you need to practise to improve your work in history.
4 Which skills in the Skills Wall are useful in other subjects?
5 Which skills in the Skills Wall are useful to employers?

I can support my argument with evidence.

I can suggest a hypothesis and use it in my work.

I know what questions to ask to check the reliability of sources.

I know how to weigh conflicting evidence to reach a conclusion.

I can explain why an event happened by discussing several reasons, not just one.

I understand why historical interpretations can change over time.

I think for myself and form my own opinions.

I can explain how changes in the past are linked to life today.

I understand that past events were not inevitable. They depended on what people decided to do.

I can work out why someone was important in history.

I understand that people's beliefs can influence their actions.

I can explain why an individual had an important effect on events.

I know that I need to understand people's motives in order to understand their actions.

◆ *Glossary*

ANGLICANS	Protestants who support the Church of England
BIGOT	someone who hates other people unfairly
BLASPHEMY	insulting God or the Church
CAVALRY	soldiers who fight on horseback
CONTROVERSIAL	causing disagreement
CRITERIA	factors to consider when making a decision or choice; standards that something is judged by
DEPOSE	overthrow
DICTATOR	a ruler with total power whose rule is based on armed force
IRONSIDE	a nickname given to Cromwell's soldiers for their bravery and determination
MUSKET	a gun with a long barrel, similar to a modern rifle
MUTINY	a protest by soldiers or sailors against their commanders, punishable by death
PLUNDER	to steal valuables, or the valuables stolen during a war like money, jewels, or even food
QUAKER	member of an extreme Puritan group which often broke up other people's church services
REBELLION	violent protests against the government
REGENT	someone appointed to rule the country during the childhood or illness of a monarch
REPUBLIC	a country without a king or queen
ROYALIST	a supporter of the King during the Civil War
TRAITOR	someone who betrays their king or country
TREASON	plotting against the king or country, punishable by death in the seventeenth century

◆ *Index*

◆ Titles in the series:

Pupils' Books (PB) and Teachers' Resource Books (TRB) are available for all titles.

◆ Acknowledgements

The Publishers would like to thank the following for permission to reproduce copyright material:

Photographs
Cover: Timepix/Mansell/Rex Features; **p.2** Chateau de Versailles, France/Bridgeman Art Library; **p.4** Private Collection/Bridgeman Art Library; **p.6** York City Art Gallery, North Yorkshire/Bridgeman Art Library; **p.11** *t* Woburn Abbey, Bedfordshire/Bridgeman Art Library, *c* Private Collection/Bridgeman Art Library; *b* Private Collection/Bridgeman Art Library; **p.14** *t* By courtesy of the National Portrait Gallery, London (NPG 1425 – detail), *c* By courtesy of the National Portrait Gallery, London (NPG 1246 – detail), *b* Burghley House Collection, Lincolnshire/Bridgeman Art Library; **p.15** Leeds Museums and Art Galleries (City Art Gallery)/Bridgeman Art Library; **p.22** *t* Jeff Parker, 2000, *c* Brian Gibbs/English Civil War Society/Topham Picturepoint, *b* Topham Picturepoint; **p.23** David Jones/Topham Picturepoint **p.31** Ashmolean Museum, Oxford; **p.35** Fotomas Index; **p.40** Timepix/Mansell/Rex Features; **p.41** *t* Private Collection/Bridgeman Art Library; **p.45** *t* © Edwin Smith (photograph: Sidney Sussex College, Cambridge), *b* Andy Butterton/PA Photos; **p.47** *top row from left:* Musée de la Tapisserie, Bayeux, France/Bridgeman Art Library, British Library, Woburn Abbey, Bedfordshire/Bridgeman Art Library, Mary Evans Picture Library, *centre row from left:* Mary Evans Picture Library, Mary Evans Picture Library/Explorer, Mary Evans Picture Library, Science Photo Library, *bottom row from left:* Hulton Archive, Peter Ruhe/ Hulton Archive, Hulton Archive, Action Press/Rex Features; **p.49** Justin Williams/The Times/NI Syndication; **p.56** *tl* By courtesy of the National Portrait Gallery, London (NPG 4691 – detail), *tc* By courtesy of the National Portrait Gallery, London (NPG 366 – detail), *tr* By courtesy of the National Portrait Gallery, London (NPG 4153 – detail), *bl* By courtesy of the National Portrait Gallery, London (NPG 544 – detail), *bc* By courtesy of the National Portrait Gallery, London (NPG 223 – detail), *br* By courtesy of the National Portrait Gallery, London (NPG 2503 – detail); **p.58** *l* By courtesy of the National Portrait Gallery, London (NPG 4691 – detail), *r* Philip Mould, Historical Portraits Ltd, London/Bridgeman Art Library; **p.59** Hulton Archive.

(*t* = top, *b* = bottom, *l* = left, *r* = right, *c* = centre)

Written sources
p.21 Barry Coward, *Oliver Cromwell*, Longman 1991; **p.25** Rosemary Sutcliff, *The Rider of the White Horse*, Hodder & Stoughton 1959; **p.35** Lyrics from 'Young Ned of the Hill' courtesy of Proper Music Group Ltd, words and music by Terry Woods and Ron Kavana; **p.49** Antonia Fraser, *Cromwell, Our Chief of Men*, Weidenfeld and Nicolson 1973.

While every effort has been made to contact copyright holders, the Publishers apologise for any omissions, which they will be pleased to rectify at the earliest opportunity.